A Lifetime Away

Childhood Memories of Stony Stratford

A Lifetime Away
Childhood Memories of Stony Stratford

Copyright © The Living Archive Project 1994

First published 1994 by Living Archive Press

Living Archive Press
The Old Bath House
205 Stratford Road
Wolverton
Milton Keynes
MK12 5RL

All rights reserved
No part of this book may be reproduced, stored in a retrieval system, or transmitted in any form or by any means, electronic, mechanical, photocopying, recording or otherwise, without prior permission of the copyright holder or in accordance with the Copyright, Design and Patents Act 1988

ISBN 0 904847 25 X

Typeset by David Lovesy of Laser Graphics, Milton Keynes
Printed by Amadeus Press, Huddersfield

Preface

This book is based on tape-recordings of Stony Stratford residents made during the research for the Living Archive Project documentary play, *Worker by Name*, which was produced in November 1992. The words are the original ones, as spoken by the interviewees.

Sifting through the transcripts of the many taped interviews, it soon became apparent that the same themes, drawn from a shared experience, kept recurring.

When the discussion turned to stories of home-life, childhood games, school, village characters and so on, similar reminiscences were triggered - an anecdote here, a name here - all adding to the picture, so that it began to feel as if I were eavesdropping on a conversation between a group of people, remembering the town where they grew up.

That is the format which I chose to relate the story of Stony Stratford during the first part of this century: the chapters appear as the collective memory of a group of older people, chatting together informally, each chipping in with snippets of information, fragments of stories overlapping and interweaving into a tapestry of childhood memories.

By today's standards, life in the early 1900's seems harsh, with the constant threat of war, the Depression and the lack of creature comforts which we take for granted nowadays. However, even when recounting stories of hardship - the boy, transported to an orphanage in a foreign country at the tender age of seven; the children who had to leave school at 14, because their parents could not afford the fees for secondary education; the families who never had a holiday; the "make do and mend" mentality - the memories are never self-pitying, but invariably philosophical.

What shines through is a feeling of being part of a close-knit community, a wonderful sense of the freedom of being a child, roaming the streets and fields around Stony, a nostalgia for the innocent pleasures of the sort of childhood which seems a life-time away.

Hilary Bell
Living Archive Project
April 1994

Acknowledgements

This book contains the recollections of:

Reg Atkins,
Betty Brassett,
Arthur Cowley,
Gladys Field,
Mrs Glave,
John Haseldine,
Audrey Lambert,
Peggy Martin,
Dorothy Meadows,
Pip Nicholls,
Alan Rose,
Iain Seymour,
Clarice Tailby,
Harold White,
Peggy Wilkinson,
Frederick Woollard.

Mr Atkins,
Peter Brazell,
Ron Eales,
Walter Franklin,
Mary Henson,
Mr King,
Dennis Lovell,
Bob Martin,
Bill Nicholls,
Bill Reynolds,
Lucy Scott,
Evelyn Sutton,
Doris Toombs,
Edward Whitehead,
Mrs Wise,

The following people recorded, transcribed and proof-read their memories:

Researchers: David Apps, Liz Burrows, Sheila Baldwin, Rib Davis, Steve Flinn, Zena Flinn, Janet Gray, Sue Haynes, Janet Irons, Roger Kitchen, Sheila Lindsay, Jean Rattenbury.

Transcribers: Hilary Bell, Herbert Booth, Sarah Cadman, Mary Cater, Jenny Daily, Rib Davis, Bill Edgar, Steve Flinn, Muriel de Grey, Margaret Halloran, Sue Haynes, Judith Jeffcoate, Roger Kitchen, Pat Morris, Lyn Pendlebury, Sue Quinn.

We are very grateful for the co-operation of contributors, who checked the facts and supplied precious photographs, and for the generosity of Brian Barnes and David and Vicki Green, who allowed us free access to their extensive collections of postcards, photographs and other memorabilia of Stony Stratford.

A family celebrates the coronation of George V in June 1911 in Russell Street.

The corner of London Road and Horsefair Green, looking south.

Home Life

Living Accommodation

There was ten of us in one house: 3 bedrooms and, of course, the usual front room, living room and kitchen. We had a big bed and there was three of us in a bed.....

We used to put bricks in the oven and wrap them in a piece of woollen blanket. When they were hot, you put them in the bed. It was lovely to get in and keep your feet warm on. There used to be three of us in that bedroom. I used to sleep against the window - the youngest ones always used to be shoved up against the window.....

It was a house with 3 bedrooms with lino on the floor and a rush mat. Pretty cold in the winter, because the winters were cold - colder than they are now. All the glass was frosted up. Originally, when we went to bed, we went with a candle, because we only had gas lights downstairs. We had brass bedsteads. I think it was an old flock mattress. When it was cold, you put a coat on the bed to keep warm. The loo was outside, so you went to the loo before you went to bed.....

We had an outside toilet with no light. In a winter's evening, we would go out with our candles, with our arm round it to stop the wind blowing it out, till we got to the toilet.....

You didn't have bathrooms either. You had a copperful every Friday night. It used to be worked out so that, either the girls were out or the boys were out but, if not, we'd hang a curtain, But nobody went in.....

We had our bath in front of the fire with the copper going and every one of us who got out, Daddy used to take down a bucket of dirty water and bring another bucket (of hot water) back. We always washed in front of the fire.....

No baths in the early days - just a tub in front of the fire and water had to be carried upstairs and carried down again after use. There was plenty of work.....

A young John Haseldine with his grandfather Jonathan in their orchard at the rear of 23 High Street (where Budgens is now).

The young Frederick Woollard with his mother.

Edwin & Agnes Franklin with their son Spencer (born in 1902) in the garden of what is now the Westminster Bank in High Street.

Of course, none of the houses in those days had bathrooms. You had to have a tin tray which you brought into the front room or in the kitchen every Friday night. You locked the back door, should anybody come up the back....

We had gas lights on the ground floor and first floor. We didn't have any light at all at the top of the house, so the people who slept on the second floor had to go to bed with candles. We had to be very careful and hold them still, so they wouldn't drip tallow all over the place.

I can still remember gas in our home. I loved it because it had a very soft glow and there was a smell and, somehow or other, it made everything cosy with the fire going as well.....

The house I lived in had linoleum on the floors and mother used to make the mats. She made the pattern up and drew it on the canvas before she started. She made them out of old coats and the like. The pictures on the walls tended to be a bit old-fashioned. We had *"The Death of Nelson"* in the front room, opposite that, we'd got *"Bubbles"*, which was quite a popular one. They had a lot of pictures of the family scattered around, as well.....

Advert from a 1930 short history of Stony Stratford.

Pickled Tongues and Corned Beef. Noted Shop for Sausages.

Phone 58.

All Home-Killed. Best Quality Meat only.

W. J. HIGGS
Family Butcher
STONY STRATFORD

Audrey Lambert, aged 3 in 1931.

Washing and Cleaning

In those days, you'd got no washing machine. You had to wait from Monday to Monday. You'd boil your water in the copper. A bath used to be filled with soft water, too, for rinsing. Then you'd have a big heavy mangle. Us children would sometimes have to turn it. They had the old Dolly tubs. If they'd got dirty clothes, especially the farmers and labourers, they used to have the dolly tubs, filled with soft water and they used to bang the clothes around with the dolly - it was like a big wooden stool, with three legs. It was all dried outside.....

Grandma always had to put her white apron on. She used to cook in a big pot, on a chain in the chimney. She used to cook her own cured bacon and broad beans, potatoes, cabbage, all in the same pot. Oh,

ARTHUR HALL'S

FAVOURITE TEA	**2s. PER LB.**
FAVOURITE TEA	
FAVOURITE TEA	A Choice blend of Indian and China Teas.
FAVOURITE TEA	
FAVOURITE TEA	Rich, Fragrant and Economical.
FAVOURITE TEA	
FAVOURITE COFFEE	**1s. 4d. PER LB.**
FAVOURITE COFFEE	
FAVOURITE COFFEE	A blend of the Finest Coffee, with a proportion of Finest Bruges Chicory.
FAVOURITE COFFEE	
FAVOURITE COFFEE	
FAVOURITE COFFEE	
FAVOURITE COCOA	**1s. PER LB.**
FAVOURITE COCOA	
FAVOURITE COCOA	Unsurpassed at the price.
FAVOURITE COCOA	
FAVOURITE COCOA	A trial will prove its superiority.
FAVOURITE COCOA	

ARTHUR HALL, STONY STRATFORD.

it was lovely! I can taste it now. They used to have a couple of pigs, sell one and keep one, so they used to hang these sides of bacon up on a wall. A couple of hams hanging up as well, always salted. When I was there, it was lovely to have a nice rasher of cured bacon and egg, not a thin rasher, it was pretty thick.

I used to go with Granny and get some butter. She'd go to a little farm down the lane and across the field to the farm and get one of those little butter-baskets and get herself a pound of butter. On her way back, she'd pick up kindling coming up the lane and put it in her bag. She had a coarse apron under her white one and she used to take her coarse apron off and put it in the front and pick up the kindling. She had an apron full of wood for the fire in the morning.....

Mother would make stew one day a week. She would also fry eggs and we had them with gravy and potatoes. She did get a joint of meat every Saturday, which we had hot on Sunday, roasted with Yorkshire pudding and vegetables, cold on Monday, as it was wash-day, and stewed on Tuesday with vegetables and dumplings. She made all sorts of milk puddings: tapioca, sago, macaroni and rice, that sort of thing. She also did suet puddings with jam or treacle. She made them in a cloth in a saucepan.....

Sometimes my mother would buy a shin of beef to make a nice stew. At weekends, we had sirloin of beef and she'd make a Yorkshire. And then sometimes in the week, sausage for a change. Of course, in those days, my father worked in the Works and he only earned fifteen and threepence. If he used to have a few pence in his pocket, he would buy a pennyworth of fish for us children from the market.

Three generations of the Meadows family, with their maid.

They didn't have all the modern things like they've got now. Mother had the old range which she cooked in and we always had a side of bacon hanging up and a bag of flour, because she used to make her own bread.

She always used to make her own cake and she always used to use vinegar instead of an egg. I suppose egg was dear and she couldn't afford it in those days. She may have put one egg and perhaps a little drop of vinegar to make up for another one. But we only had cake once a week.....

For twopence (1p), you could get offal: liver, heart, scrag-end of lamb or a little bit of meat. You could get corned beef. Mum used to make "Bucks Clangers": they're a suet pudding with potato, meat and bits of onion, tied in a cloth and boiled. Mother made hers with corned beef, because bacon was so dear.....

You've never lived unless you've had a cured pig in the house. We cured them ourselves in the lead and salt - salt petre. We used to stick in the knuckles of the bones, cured and salted, keep them turned in the brine, keep covering the brine over and hang them up to dry and then wrap them. I fitted some hooks upstairs and they used to hang up there. After they had hung for a few months, you could start to eat them. They were massive things. Hell of a weight. You had to ceremoniously cut a piece off. That used to be about 2 inches of fat. Fat that had gone yellow and about half an inch, at the most, were lean. And it had gone hard as this fireplace here. When you put that in the frying pan (I'm not exaggerating, if I say you had half inch of fat in there). Gawd, you'd never lived until you'd had that for breakfast! You used to chuck big thick slices of bread in the fat and fry it. We always used to eat food like that. Everybody tells us we can't now.

After we'd been pig killing, we used to have all the meat and odd bits and pieces of meat and things you couldn't eat. My mother used to spend days having it in the oven to render it down to get the lard off it. There was bucketfuls of it to be eaten over the next winter. We used to do the pig killing in the autumn. Then there was a lot of that used to go in - bacon and onion - to what used to be called the "Buckinghamshire Clanger". I never could stand that.....

A bill from Odells for domestic supplies to the Higgs family, September 1928.

We used to have the old-fashioned fireplaces with black hobs and we used to put a great big saucepan on there and we was never without food. We always had bread and there was always cups hanging up, so if us children was hungry, we could go in and we'd got soup.

We used to have lots of bread and dripping. Bread and lard with sugar on. That was when the butchers used to make their own lard. They used to make the lard in big trays and stand it outside, so that it frosted and then they'd bring it back in and you could buy it. Beautiful.....

We used to deliver on our horse and cart to Deanshanger. Me dad would always stop at the butchers there, bring back a sheep's head for dinner. It looked like a sheep's head, you'd just take its eyes out, that's all. You split it down the middle, so you'd got two halves and then you just put it in a stew jar, with your carrots, onions and all the other bits that go into a stew.....

Other people, who hadn't got quite the same facilities, used to take their Christmas dinner down to the baker to be cooked. In fact my first father-in-law always took their turkey to Arthur Cowley's to be cooked and fetched it back at a quarter to one. They had to book it, so that he'd have space in the oven, which was where he cooked the bread. All the rest of the year, he would cook the Yorkshire puddings for their Sunday dinner. When we were coming back from our walks, we would see people coming along, with their tin trays and a cloth over the top, with their Yorkshire pudding in it. My grandparents would have a huge one - about a foot long by about 8 inches and, between the two of them, they would eat the lot before their main course. Just eat it plain, as it was.....

Grandpa used to make hop beer in a barrel in the wash house. He used to go out with his half-pint glass at night - that was a horned glass. Gran used to make a lot of wine - cowslip for keeping and parsnip for drinking. Down the lane where we used to go, there was a field full of cowslips and I used to go down and pick them.....

Everybody made home-made wine, that's all they could afford to drink.....

Arthur Cowley on the baker's cart, with Taffy the horse, 1935.

Mr Meadows in his orchard in what is now Cofferidge Close

Self Sufficiency

There was a very great shortage of jobs round here and virtually everybody had a big allotment. Everything you wanted came off that. We were totally self-sufficient for greenstuffs and potatoes, winter and summer alike. Frankly, what didn't come off there, you didn't have.....

We never wanted for fruit. We lived in plenty in that respect. Father grew everthing. Mother never bought anything in a tin, well maybe on Sunday. We never bought vegetables from a tin. Mother bottled plums and apples and we had fruit pies all the year round, and jam. There was enough jam to last us all year.....

I have very happy memories of our orchard. There were trees all around. We almost lived on apples during the season - apple pie, apple dumpling, stewed apple in all sorts of puddings. We had quite a variety of apples: Coddling, Beauty of Bath, Coxes Orange Pippin, Warner's King. They all had their different seasons. Some of them were keepers and were put in the stable-loft and we also had a shed at the back of the shop, where there was a loft and they were laid out carefully on straw and kept for the winter.

My father used to bring apples out on to the Green and throw them out and children would rush for them and take them home for their mothers. But we really had quite a quantity and they were sold to Northampton shops and they had to be gathered very carefully, so that they were not bruised.....

We used to go and collect manure and leaves. We used to sweep up all the leaves and put them into a truck and it was all mixed up and it used to go up the allotments and Daddy used to grow all his own vegetables and flowers.....

During the War, when my parents had poultry, I would take two huge buckets each day to my school (York House) and collect from the kitchen, all the potato peelings and other kitchen scraps. Then I would call at about four houses along here as well, with all these buckets. At the same point in the War, they used to put tin baths in the street for the residents to put all their stuff in and then people, like my parents, could buy this bathful of stuff each week to cook and feed to the poultry.....

My sister helped with the housework and the cooking. I was always helping my father. Out of the back of the house, we had two pens: there was laying hens in one and cockerels in the other. They had to be cleaned out and these pens were very high. You didn't need asking who was going to go in there! If you've been in the pen with some cockerels a few weeks before Christmas, they were fighting fit. There was no caponising then, they were full-blown cockerels. If you'd been in there on your hands and knees to clean them out, you knew what cockerels were!

There was one thing I shall never forget as long as I live: I came home from work one day and I notices a rabbit hutch in the garden with a rabbit in there. It was a young'un - a Belgian Giant. After a week or two, more hutches appeared and more rabbits. We kept having these rabbits and playing with them, they were pets. This Belgian thing got to a hell of a size - it must have been about 8 or 9 pounds.

My Dad calmly comes up to me one day and says, "Kill that rabbit boy. We'll have that for dinner on Sunday." It was the first time I ever answered my father back. "I'm not. You kill him." We had a fair old row about it and, in the finish, next time I went home from work, he'd got a pal of his to do it. It was killed, skinned and hung up. My Dad decided he was going to have him stuffed and roasted and, Sunday dinner time, there lays the rabbit. The table was laid, vegetables, gravy out. We all four of us sat and looked at it. None of us had any dinner. That rabbit just disappeared. Next day, when I came home from work at night, all the rabbits had gone, the hutches had gone and all the rabbit food was gone. I never did know where they went. So that was the end of that.....

By the time I was nine, the War started and food changed. Father kept rabbits and he would kill a rabbit every week and consequently, I don't like rabbit any more. He also kept pigeons for a while, but they were more expensive to feed so we didn't have them for long.....

IF YOU REQUIRE A GOOD, USEFUL, ECONOMICAL TEA, USE ONLY

"THE FAVOURITE TEA"

PER 2s. LB.

IT IS SURE TO GIVE SATISFACTION.

And if you require an absolutely Pure Baking Powder, that you can use **without fear of Indigestion,** use the

"Medicated Fruit Baking Powder,"

PER 1s. LB.

THE INCREASING SALE OF WHICH PROVES ITS SUPERIORITY OVER ALL OTHERS. TO BE HAD ONLY OF

ARTHUR HALL,

STONY STRATFORD.

We used to have a lot of rabbits: anybody who went rabbiting on Sunday morning would get 50 or 60 rabbits, no trouble at all. They were sixpence each and then there was a rag and bone dealer come round and give you 3d for the skin.....

We used to go and get eels for dinner. There used to be two big grills in the river and they were the eel traps. When the young eels got in there, they couldn't get back out. So we used to go down there and get eels. Eel pie, beautiful.....

We kept all sorts of fowl: chickens, geese, ducks. We used to have a few Rhode Island Reds and you'd get cross-breeds come out, because we didn't keep them in pens. They were free-roaming, so you couldn't really keep any particular breed. You might start off with one, but you would lose it. We always used to have a Michaelmas goose.

We used to keep pigs and sell pigs; we always had a pig or two about the place. There was a chap called Alf Smith, used to work for Canvin's, the Butchers. He used to come on Sunday morning and get his noose and slip it behind the pig's back teeth. Naturally, the pig wanted to pull backwards, but you pulled him out by force. He'd have

Dennis Lovell age 17, his sister Ruth, with evacuee, and his mother Mrs E. Lovell.

a humane killer - that's like a pistol, only it doesn't shoot a bullet, it shoots a spike out. He put it behind his forehead and that stunned him and then you cut his throat. You'd catch the blood then for black puddings. You had to be a bit smart with the bowl.

Then you'd got a big pile of wheatstraw by the side: you put the carcass on that and set fire to it, to burn the bristles off. You turned him over and burned the other side off. Then you'd get him on the "Scratch", which was a piece of kit, like a table with four handles on it, at each corner. You'd have plenty of hot water and a scraper and you'd get him clean. You'd take his nails off his claws. There was a little hook on the back

Betty, Josie, Vera & Peggy Scragg, in 1931.

of the scraper and you'd get the hook behind the nail and pull them off because, once they'd been in the fire, they were loosened off. You got him cleaned, you hoisted him up in the air and slit him down the middle and took his insides out and that was it for the day. You'd leave him to cool.

Then Alf would come back the next day to joint him up and then the only problem was the insides: you'd got the chitterlings (intestines) you'd got the pig's pluck (heart and lungs). You used every bit of it. The only bit of a pig you didn't use was its squeak - its voice box.

You used to cut up the chitterlings into suitable lengths, squeeze all the rubbish out of the inside. Then you'd turn them inside out on a bit of bamboo. Slide the bamboo up, turn it over and pull 'em back out, and keep washing 'em in salt water till you got 'em thoroughly clean, then you used to have 'em fried. The pig's pluck, you made into faggots. We made black puddings with the blood we saved. You just put salt with it to stop it congealing, then you mix it with groats and penny royal (that's your seasoning) put it in skins and boil it.

We did our own salting: salted the hams and of course, there's some pieces, like spare ribs that you had to eat straight away, 'cause, you've got to remember, there weren't any deep freezers then.

You wouldn't kill a pig then, not unless it had got to about 20 score or something like that (20 pounds in a score), but they're about 8 score when they kill 'em now. You'd only kill about twice a year, when there's an 'R' in the month.

The trotters were used for pork hock, it makes them thicken up. Got a lot of little bones in it mind you, you've got to be careful of those. The pig's head you could make into brawn and pork pie. You had to eat it pretty quick because, like I say, no fridges.

The Diamond Wedding of Daniel and Harriet Cowley, May 1929.

Back row (left to right): Mrs Kathy Cowley, Mr & Mrs Rogers, Alan Cowley, Mr & Mrs Philpotts
Mid row: Mrs George Cowley, Mr & Mrs Rogers' Daughter, Harry Cowley, Harriet Cowley,
Daniel Cowley, Hugh & Lillian Cowley with son Arthur on her knees
Front row: Charles, James & Mary Rogers, Peter Philpotts, Dorothy Rogers

Once you'd got your hams salted up in the brine, you used to put 'em up over the oven to dry. Once you'd got 'em dry, they were as hard as bullets and the pigs then was about twice as big as the pigs today.....

Make Do and Mend

I can remember my father mending all of our shoes. He always sat on the rag rug in front of the fire. He used to buy a big sheet of leather down the *Old George Yard* from the Tanning Factory....

My Dad used to get a piece of cardboard and put it in the bottom of his shoes and hob nails. I used to wear little black patent ankle strap shoes and as soon as I'd been to the shop and fetched them my Dad used to set to and he'd put big hob nails all the way round so they lasted and then the cardboard was for warmth.....

Up until I left school, mother made most of my clothes and she made my coats. I always used to make a fuss about the little hat she used to make 'cause they used to be in panels, little hats in panels with a little brim and sometimes they were very tight and squeezed my ears. She was quite a good seamstress, I suppose, she made my sisters' coats in their days.....

In winter, your Mum always used to learn you to knit, sew, crochet, make carpets and things like that - the big old rag rugs. In the summer, you used to be with your Dad.....

Environment

Our bedroom was at the front of the house and that was six feet from the traffic. The lorries in those days mostly had solid tyres and they always had chunks out of them, so all through the night you got the vibration of lorries and the rattle and banging of them. Cups and saucers used to rattle on the table when the traffic went by. Then the Powers-that-be had the road up and put a concrete base in and put wooden blocks in that were about 3 inches wide and about 9 inches long, stood on their ends and packed tight. On that went a rubberised surface, the idea being that it would stop the noise. It did, but the lorries couldn't stop on it. They used to come down Old Stratford in them days and when they started braking to come into the town at the 10 mile an hour limit, they didn't stop. They used to skid. Pitham's house was across the way and they had many a one through their front window, just smashed right in. So the rubberised surface had to come up and they put grit in.....

Removing the tram lines from Wolverton Road after the tram ceased operating in 1926.

Flooding in High Street.

Just before the War, a lorry carrying Sunlight soap caught fire at the top of the hill. My father worked at the garage and we had Sunlight soap for years after that and we weren't the only ones in Stony!....

I can always remember about the flooding. It flooded right from the bridge at Old Stratford; it used to come in from across what was the A5, straight down until the other side of the Orphanage. They couldn't get down with any buses or anything, but one of the farmers had got carts out with trestles on and we paid them to progress through the floods. That went on every year until they altered the river.....

We used to have floods around the bottom end of the High Street, this side of the Orphanage. I used to live in the terrace and used to keep watch on it. You'd see it creeping up and get into the kitchen and then into the living room and the front room, but we used to move our stuff upstairs and to get from the house to the High Street, you had no wellingtons in them days, you'd walk on chairs, step on one and pull the other one in front. If you didn't want to walk through the water and you wanted to go up the street you'd have to take your shoes and socks off, pull your trousers up.

The mail used to come from Deanshanger in the covered wagon and they used to shout out as they come through, "The floods are up." And my father would say, "Come on, the floods are up." So we'd have to start doing something about it.

I knew the road when it was mud and stones and I saw it concreted and wooden blocks put on. The water would fetch them up - the water couldn't get away and they started swelling and stood as much as they could and then they started coming up. That was the end of the wooden blocks.

The Council used to spray the road in the summer with water. The cart used to go round and spray and keep the dust down. There was some dust in them days. You talk about hygiene, all the windows to the butchers' shops were open with all the dust. Nobody ever died from meat poisoning, as far as I know.....

My wife and I often mention how, in the summertime, in the main street, when it had rained, with the heat of the sun on it, the smell that came off it was a smell you'll never ever forget and, after a shower, now, you say, "That's not like the smell it used to be.".....

Everybody was friendly and helped each other. Nobody locked doors. When the weather was hot, you opened the front door and the back door and just let the breeze flow through. Very often the men would sit on the doorstep and puff their pipes and have a little talk in the street.

Paperhangings! Paperhangings!! Paperhangings!!!

J. PACEY,

STONY STRATFORD,

HAS JUST RECEIVED A

New & Select Stock for the Present Season at very Low Prices.

A General Assortment of Fancy Cabinet and Household Furniture always on hand.

LINOLEUM AND OIL FLOOR CLOTHS. COCOA, MANILLA, and other MATTINGS IN GREAT VARIETY.

AN INSPECTION IS INVITED.

The wedding of Joe Eld from Coventry & Mrs Franklin's niece Miss Kingston in 1911/12. Taken in the garden behind 26 Wolverton Road at John Franklin's house. The vicar is Rev. Moxon. The baby in his father's arms on the far right of the second row from the back is Walter Franklin, aged about 1.

Stony Stratford celebrates Empire Day in the Market Square, 1908.

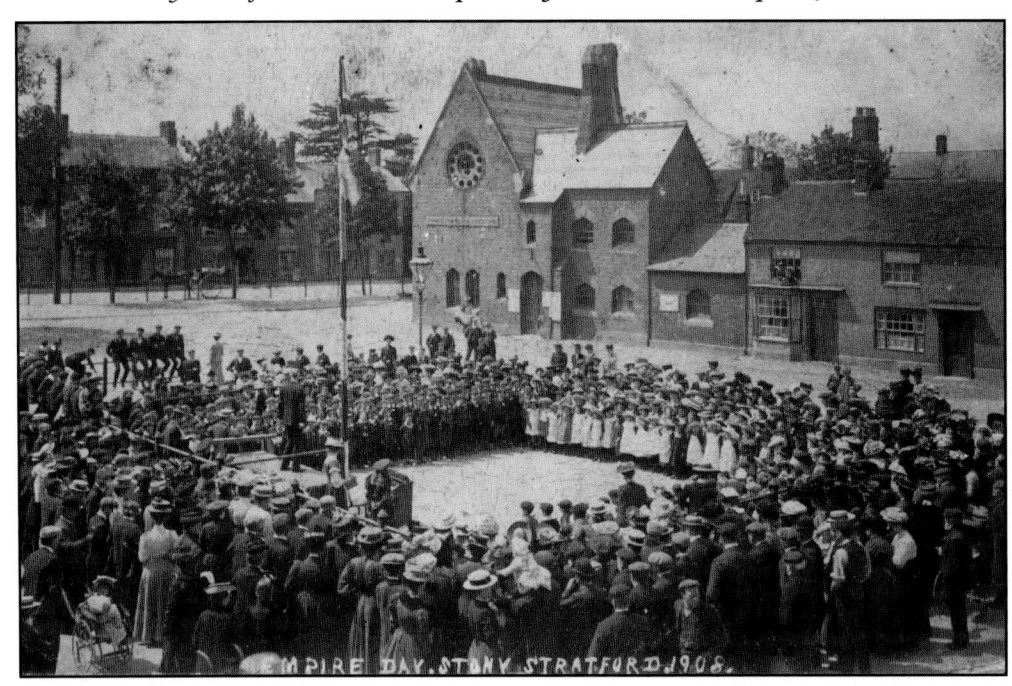

Stony Stratford celebrates the Coronation of Edward VII in 1902.

Schooldays

The British School on the right hand corner, looking north down the High Street, circa 1908.

The British School

When I was a little girl of five, I used to have to walk from Old Stratford to the corner of Stony Stratford, where the old Public Hall was.....

The Public Hall was always called the British School - the Non-Conformist School. The School was a trust, founded by members of the Baptist and Congregational Churches.....

The School in the Public Hall used to be one, huge class-room, with a hot stove in the middle with different classes and different teachers, all in this one room.

We used to have to rest with our heads on the little table, when we were small - half an hour's rest. We had a governess for the little ones. They were very strict, but very nice and kind. We never came out to the playground, all of a rush, like they do now. We used to file out quietly. We had a morning prayer and hymn and evening prayer and hymn, when we left.

If I was late for school, Mummy used to say, "Get your hoop." The boys had an iron hoop with a hook on it and we had a wooden hoop. We'd whip them up, because we could then, there was no traffic.

Russell Street School

When I was seven, the Russell Street School was built. I remember I was one of the first to be marched round there. The first day at Russell School was fascinating, because they had an Assembly Hall and taps and proper lavatories with running water. I'd never seen a tap before so, going to school and turning the tap on, it fascinated me. I thought that everything was wonderful.

There were three Infant classes and there were five Standards. When you got to the Fifth, you couldn't go any further, you were stuck.

All the girls had to wear pinafores; the boys just wore ordinary clothes with bows and celluloid collars that could be sponged.

On Empire Day, the whole school used to go out into the playground and sing the songs of the Empire, with the flags. Any eclipses - we used to go out. The teachers used to have smoked glass to see through.

We had a lot of history too, all about the Empire. There was a lot to learn in those days. They used to teach what they don't teach now: you had a sewing mistress and a music teacher. The boys had carpentry classes. Now, the children don't know how to sew. They use all these computers, they'll never learn to add up like we used to.....

We used to have a nice big lawn out the back of Russell Street School. There was quite a big playground. There was a big orchard. We used to have Sports Day on the lawn at school and in the playground - races up and down.....

The boys and girls had to play separately. You couldn't mix. The boys' playground was there and the girls' playground was there, you were never allowed to play together. You could be together in the classrooms, but you mustn't play together.....

The brand new Russell Street School, from a postcard dated 1908.

The Girls' playground at St Mary's School (now The Plough public house), circa 1924.

Headmistress E.M.L. Plumb's class at St Mary's School, sometime in the early 1930's.

There were three schools operating then, the Russell Street Primary School, run by the Council, and the Boys' School and Girls' School, both run by the Church.....

The girls went to St Mary's and the boys went to St Giles'. As far as the Council School was concerned - never the twain shall meet - it was always them and us.

St Mary's and St Giles' Schools

The Infant School was St Mary's, where *The Plough* pub is now. The girls stayed at St Mary's School and the boys stayed until we was about 7 and then you came down the High Street to St Giles' until you left school.....

I started school where *The Plough* is now, when I was about four and we used to sit in school chairs, baby chairs and have slates and sandboards (you know, like a tray with sand in) and we used to draw in the sand with a stick or something, like kids do at the seaside.....

I had lots of friends around in Clarence Road. We were a group who played together and grew up together and most of my friends came with me to St Mary's School. In those days, the Headmistress was Miss Plumb, the Governess. I think I started school at four and a half. I can remember that winter quite well. That particular winter was very snowy. I was a bit of a naughty girl: I used to run away from school. I was a very nervous child and my parents had a lot of trouble with me. I can remember one particular incident: in Wolverton Road, at the top opposite Clarence Road, there used to be a little family grocer's shop, run by a Mr Dickens and his two sons.....

I'd run away from school and, of course, Mother didn't know and it was very cold and there was no use going home until it was four o'clock, but I couldn't tell the time so, every few minutes, I'd pass the shop and I'd go inside and say, "Mr Dickens, is it four o'clock yet?" "No, it isn't", he'd say. This went on for quite a bit until, in the end, he called me in and gave me a biscuit. I think I got warm in the shop. But he never did let me forget that. He would remind me for years afterwards, about the time when he said I'd "played the wag"!.....

A group of local children outside Dickens' Shop

An outing from St Mary's School to Windsor. Mary Henson is on the far left in the front row.

There used to be more children to a class. Half of you used to take it in turns and stand at the back of the class and do your lessons with the slates. Nobody thought there was anything wrong with it. We learnt just the same......

Our teachers dressed very old-fashioned. Miss Plumb, the Governess, had her little black velvet bit round her neck with a cameo and they wore woolly stockings. They were rather old-fashioned, even for the times. They were very strict with us girls and we did an awful lot of pillow lace. Some of the girls made a beautiful altar cloth for St Mary's Church on the London Road. I might add that none of my work went into it; my work was always grubby.

I wasn't all that good at arithmetic, but I think our Headmistress had a funny way of teaching us: she would work out a sum on the board and we would join in with her. Well, there were probably three or four bright girls who knew what they were doing. The rest of us chatted and joined in, you see. The sum was obviously right, because we had done it together.

We used to have two vicars come in from St Mary's and St. Giles' Churches to give us a talk and a lesson once a week. The St Giles' Vicar was the Reverend Steer and the St Mary's was the Reverend Payne. He used to be portly - a rather fattish man - we used to nickname him "Tubby" Payne.

I remember on Empire Day, we were encouraged to put daisies in our button holes and we would stand in the playground and salute the Union Jack Flag. Being a Church school, we used to go to Church on Ash Wednesday, first thing in the morning at 9 o'clock. Of course, we liked that because it gave us an hour or two off lessons. And on Shrove Tuesday and Ascension Day we had half day.....

I can remember, when I was at school, we used to take eggs to school, ordinary, new-laid eggs and they put your name on and they used to send them off to the troops. I've got a photo of one fellow in the Army who's got his arm in a sling and he sent me a photo 'cause he had my egg with my name on.....

I went to St Mary's from about age four till eight. The first time I got into trouble was when I daren't run through the girls' playground, 'cause the girls were so big. I were dying for a pee, so I peed in the corner and then we had to line up to go back to class. The Teacher said, "And who's responsible for that?" Of course, Muggins puts his hand up, so I got a telling off for that.....

At school, we seemed to have these funny toilets: they were wooden seats and they seemed to have a pipe going all along and it flushed the lot.....

The teacher sat up at a high desk on a high stool and, if we were in the front row, we used to drop a rubber as near as we could, so we could get under her desk and look up her clothes!....

The teacher was very nice. I remember she used to make us daisy chains if we were good. She'd say, "Well, you can have a daisy chain today."

We used to have concerts in the playground and then people used to come round the railings and watch us. But, nearly always, I used to take a boy's part. I can remember the governess saying, "Oh Dear, you ought to have been a boy." I said, "Well it's your fault, you always give me boys' parts!"....

My sisters went to St Mary's the whole of their school days, but, being a boy, I had to move down the High Street to St Giles' School.....

We done more reading than anything because, as time went on, we got to the War Years and it was a job to get teachers then, so they used to say, "private reading", so you used to get the books out and sit and read.....

Mr Toms, the Headmaster, was the organist at St Giles' Church. He was a short man. I don't know whether he was an operaphile, but he would have two or three classes in the school hall and we would sing things like *"On with the Motley"*, and *"The Toreador's Song"* from *"Carmen"*. We learnt them all off by heart. There was no music. He would read out the words, play the piano and say, "Sing." I can sing you them now. I love music now and I am sure that is where I got it from.....

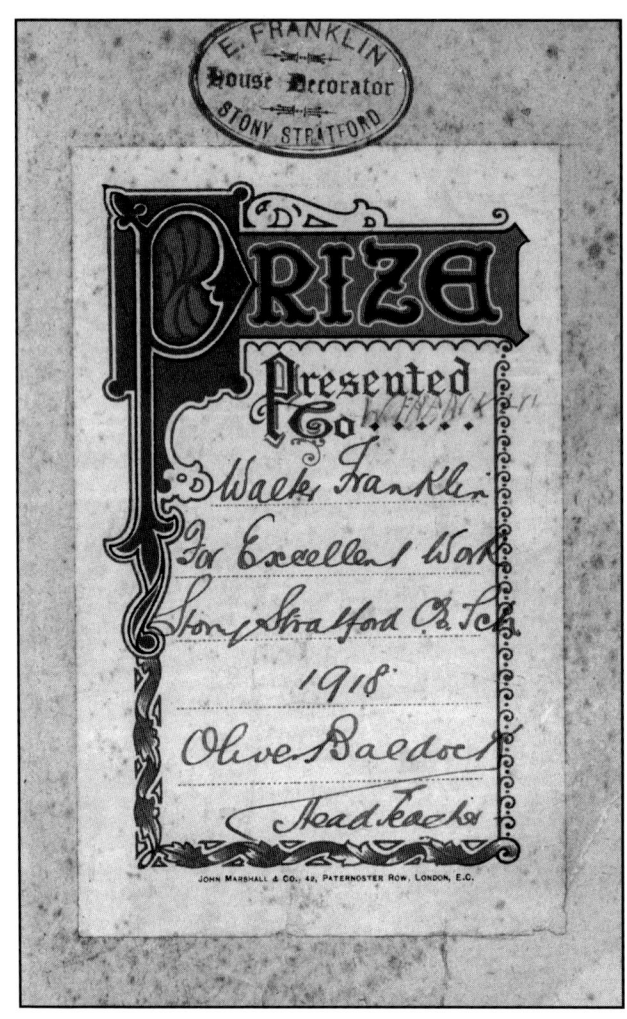

High Street showing St Giles' School - the second building up on the right hand side, circa 1907.

St Giles' School pupils, 1910, with Oliver Baldock, Headmaster, on the far right of the second row. Miss Plumb is on the left. Among the boys, in the middle of the front row, is Billy Alderman, later known as "Cinder" Billy. On the second row on the far right is Spencer Franklin.

St Giles' School, circa 1922. (Left to right) Back Row: Harry Plum, Harold Ford, Bill Frost, Stan Dixon, Fred Savage, Jack Dixie, "Journey" Pearson, Harry Wildman. Middle Row: Ted Nicholls, Arthur Eaton, Willie Toms (Headmaster), John Wildman, William Warren. Front Row: Walter Franklin, Bill Bromley, Billy Brown, Bert Bonham, Roy Humphries.

On our Syllabus, in the winter it was allotments and gardening in the summer. After the Easter holidays, it was swimming.....

We didn't wear uniform, but it was a darnsight more formal than it is today. There weren't many children who left school in those days, who couldn't read and write. I got no punishment at school, perhaps I was a goody-goody, although I don't think I was any different from anyone else. If you deserved punishment, you got it - a clout round the head, whether it did you brain damage or not and I don't think it did that to anybody, to be quite frank.....

When I went to St Giles', the first two or three years, the Headmaster was Oliver Baldock - he was a sod. He was never without a cane and he didn't take many steps before he clouted someone with it.

We were in what they called the Library, upstairs. It was a big room with hardly anything in it - a few forms and a stack of books and we'd got a fire up there, 'cause the boilers had broke down. He sat by the fire and we done some recitation and we sung some songs and then he asked if anybody would sing a solo. A little orphan boy, named Willy Warburton, from up the Wolverton Road said, "Yes, I'll sing a song," He weren't very tall, he was a cockney. "I'll give him thruppence." Baldock said. (Well, blimey, that isn't the Oliver Baldock I know). So Little Billy comes out and he sings a Cockney song and we all cheered and laughed and clapped and he went up for his thruppence. Baldock said, "I've changed my mind. I'll give you three pen'orth of the best," And he gave him three or four slashes across the back and sent him back. Rotten sod, wasn't he?....

When I was eight or nine at St Giles' School, we used to come out of the back of the school into Russell Street, along Vicarage Walk, through the Recreation Ground and into Queen Street. It was impossible for the school-children to play football on the Recreation Ground after school, because the pitches were being used by the unemployed.....

The first winners of the Bird and Tree Competition for Buckinghamshire, circa 1902.
(Left to right) Back row: O. Baldock (Headmaster of St Giles'), Miss Fryer (Headmistress of St Mary's), Rev H. Last (Vicar of St Giles' Church).
Middle Row: Frank Webster, Sidney Dumbleton, Percy Diamond, Albert French.
Front Row: Annie Negus, Arthur Garrett, Ruth Bennett, Sidney Millward, Winnie Kightley.

St Giles' School, 1928.
(Left to right) Back Row: Bill Goodyer, George Webb, ?
3rd Row: Mr Toms, Jim Bimson, Frank Abbott, Bernard Daniels, - Read, Ken Sanford, Tom Dicks.
2nd Row: - James, Rod Dearn.
Front Row: Tim Bramley, - Clarke, ?, - Cordell, ?

We used to have a nit nurse, Nurse Grey. She used to come every so often and my mum was pretty quick on that. If she saw you scratching your head, she'd say, "Come on.", and get a very fine comb to see. We used to line up and walk past Nurse Grey. She must have known my mother 'cause, when I got to her, she used to put her hand on my shoulder and push me along. But those that she did find something on , had to stand on one side and then the mother had a note saying that their child had nits, so I think they had to be washed with carbolic soap and paraffin.....

We used to have Horlicks, not milk, at breaktime in the mornings.....

Some of the children used to walk right in from Beachampton and Calverton, but there was no dinner at school, they used to take sandwiches.....

The new St Mary's and St Giles' School in Queen Street was opened in 1937 and that was paid for by donations and collections by the two churches and that school didn't cost the County Council a halfpenny. I can remember, I was in the Choir at the time and the Reverend Payne appealed in the pulpit for the people to pay so much a week. My mother paid sixpence a week for fifty two weeks. Doesn't sound much now, but that was an awful lot of money in the Thirties. She was one of the many who did that. There is a roll somewhere in excess of three hundred and that was done by the two churches.....

For the last twelve months of my schooling, they built the new school, so we did our last year at school there in 1937, but most of the time was spent gardening or doing odd jobs to turn it into a school.....

St Giles' and St Mary's were Church of England Schools and, when they opened that school down by the Sports Field, they closed. I think I only did one year at St Giles', before it closed, then we had to go to the Council School in Russell Street. It was something to do with the Education Act.....

You went to the Council School till you passed your Eleven Plus and then you went to Wolverton Grammar School; if you didn't pass, you went down to the new Church School, which was a Secondary Modern.....

The builders outside the newly completed St Mary's & St Giles' School.

I can't really say that I did like school. There were things we were supposed to be taught that I never did know what they were talking about. One thing - I've got a deep dislike of poetry. Cannot abide poetry in any fashion at all. That all comes from school. God knows what they were supposed to be teaching us. I fail to know even now. Every week, we had one session of reading this poem, "....a host of golden daffodils." "I wandered lonely as a cloud..." You know the one I mean. Every week the same thing, the same few lines being read. God knows what we were supposed to be learning, but I hated that.....

We used to learn long tracts of poetry which they don't do today. I think of winter afternoons, because we still had gas light in schools in those days, and of saying "*Lucy Gray*" and it takes me back to those afternoons in the wintertime and I've always retained a great interest in poetry because of what I learned at school.....

York House School

Just before five, I went to the York House School, just around the corner, which is now the Youth Club. I continued at the school until I was 14. Life for me was perhaps a little different from some of the other girls in Stony Stratford because I went to private school and tended not to know many of the local girls. My friends were all boarders who came from far and wide. I would go up some Saturdays, just to play with them.

The School cost Father £9 a term around 1933, but I don't know how much the boarders paid. As it was a private school, I didn't have to sit an entrance exam. They only took boys up to the age of ten. Some played up and I think they were glad when they left. I think, to begin with, the education there was better than other

York House School, London Road, Circa 1908.

schools, because it had very small classes, about twelve or fifteen in each, with about 150 altogether in the school.

I was a day girl at the school, because I only had to come from around the corner, but there were weekly boarders. A lot of them were farmers' daughters and business people's daughters, even locally, like the jewellers or the builders and quite a number of foremen's daughters from the Railway Works.

I actually started the term, when the two Miss Slades retired and Mrs Ogilvie came to run the school in September 1933. The school uniform colours were 'Saxe' blue, navy and white. The blazer was striped,

The front of York House in the Summer, with the pupils working outside.

whereas the dresses would be in saxe blue with navy and white dots on it. You also had a navy gymslip and white blouses in winter, with a striped tie. Part of the uniform was black lace-up shoes to go to school and when you got there you had a locker and changed into shoes, which had a button. These were house shoes. One of the first things you learnt was how to tie up shoes and how to button up your shoes. You used a wooden frame with canvas on top, with two tapes about six in a row, so you could do six bows or buttons.

We did do some sewing, but they didn't seem to dwell on it too much. I can remember making my own pairs of knickers, in the same pattern of the dresses of course, so that they matched. Also, we would have to wear what we called "ETB's" - elastic tops and bottoms, which tended to come below one's skirt. These things had to cover your black stocking-tops, so you hadn't any gaps.

York House School

BOARDING AND DAY SCHOOL FOR GIRLS & YOUNG BOYS :: :: :: ::

Preparation for Public Examinations. Senior, Junior, Kindergarten and Nursery Departments. :: Moderate Inclusive Fees :: ::

Stony Stratford

One thing I really enjoyed was, once a year, they had to have a fire drill. For a day girl like me, it was optional. For the boarders, it was compulsory and quite a number of them used to scream their heads off when they were made to do this. It was a three-storey building and there was a huge firehose stuck on the wall near one of the side windows and you were then strapped on this thing by the teacher. The window, of course, was open and she would push you off the window cill. This is the point where most of them screamed their heads off. Then she would let you down and you had to pad the wall with your hands, all the way down to the bottom. There was another teacher at the bottom, waiting to unstrap you. If you were lucky, like me, I would hare up three flights of stairs to see if I could get in the queue and have another go!

I think we were well off, in comparison with other people. I did feel different from the other children, because they used to shout after me in the street. This did worry me at times.....

York House has changed completely. I can't tell you what it was like. It was a lovely place in those days: lovely gardens and playing fields at the back. Miss Dorothy Slade was the Headmistress and her sister taught music. Every term there would be some sort of 'Do'. I used to play the piano and, with somebody else, a duet. People said pieces of poetry and there was singing.....

Secondary Education

To get to Higher Education, in those days, you had to win a scholarship. You either went to the Technical or the Apprentice School. The Grammar School was in Wolverton.....

You did have the opportunity of taking an exam to go to the two Senior Schools in Wolverton, or the Technical College. Your parents had to pay £5 a year in fees and my mother and father hadn't got it. Simple as that.....

A class photo at Stony Stratford Secondary School, 1950.

I went to the Grammar in Wolverton at eleven. Of course, it was the days of fee-paying then: £4.11s (£4.55p) a year, which was quite a lot, when the average weekly wage would probably be 50/- (£2.50p), something like that.....

For eighteen months, I went to Wolverton Secondary School in Moon Street. We used to go up on the tram and fight all the Wolverton boys. Got many a black eye and gave many a black eye. Very pugilistic, looking back.....

My school days were happy. I loved school and I was one of the top scholars. I wasn't so keen when I went to the Technical at Wolverton. That was the start of adult life, homework, etc. At the Tech., we had typing, book-keeping, commerce and geography, shorthand, history, needlework, cookery.....

After I left school, I started going to night school at Wolverton. We went to the old Science and Arts in Church Street, opposite where the Post Office is now. I reckon I learnt more in the three or four years after I left school than ever I did when I was there.

Looking along Wolverton Road, 1921.

St Giles' Church, showing "Donkey" Hall's shop, before demolition.

The High Street entrance to Fegan's Homes during a flood, in the 1930's.

The rear view of Fegan's Homes from a 1906 postcard.

Fegan's Homes

Arriving

I was sent over to Stony Stratford just before I reached my 7th birthday. I remember coming down to London. I remember clinging on to my foster mother, Mrs Duncan's, coat because I was so afraid of the traffic, not being used to that in County Wicklow where you hardly saw a car, let alone anything else.

I remember it was a very hot day and Mr Walmsley, an old Fegan's boy, who became the General Superintendent, brought me to Stony Stratford. Then I remember Mr Walmsley taking me over to the Chapel. I came on a Saturday and Mr and Mrs Bennett were preparing for the following day's service, which was Harvest Festival. I remember Mr Bennett saying, "Johnny, this is your new Mummy."

Well I cried when I first came and I felt, "Here I am in this foreign land with all these boys, 150 of them." Some were good and some were bullies and I know, the first week I was there, I felt awful and I cried. Mrs Bennett treated me as something special, as I was the youngest boy at the time, and she used to come up and dress me and wash me and I used to get called a pet, which I was.

Fegan's Chapel decorated for Harvest Festival, 1937.

Iain "Johnny" Seymour, aged 9, dressed in Sunday best. The bow tie was on elastic and when it was weak, it broke when you sneezed.

Daily chores

I think we got up at 7 o'clock and went downstairs to the wash-place, where you washed in icy cold water, except at Christmas, and when that was done, we had our breakfast. It was one thick slice of bread and margarine or bread and dripping and one cup of tea and, in winter, you had porridge. Occasionally, you had a dose of Epsom Salts or liquorice powder and then you went upstairs and made your bed. You'd get this cloth with a big, heavy weight on a pole - you know, the old bumper - and polish the dormitory.

In one of the dormitories, there was a part of the dormitory where all the boys who used to wet the bed consistently, used to be made to sleep on straw mattresses and, once a week, they would have to go down and change their straw in the pigsty and get fresh straw and bring it back up.

Uniform

You had grey serge shorts and they were lined with flannel, so that you did not have to wear pants. Then you wore black stockings and black boots and you had slippers, when you were off duty. Then you had a fine blue and white striped shirt and a blue wool jersey. Then a grey serge jacket which buttoned up like a soldier's uniform. You were not allowed to have any gloves, oh no! Then on Sundays, when you went to Chapel, you wore a dog-collar, like an Eton collar. How we used to hate those. You could scrub them. Then there was a black bow with a little elastic loop, which you buttoned on to your stud.

East end dorm.

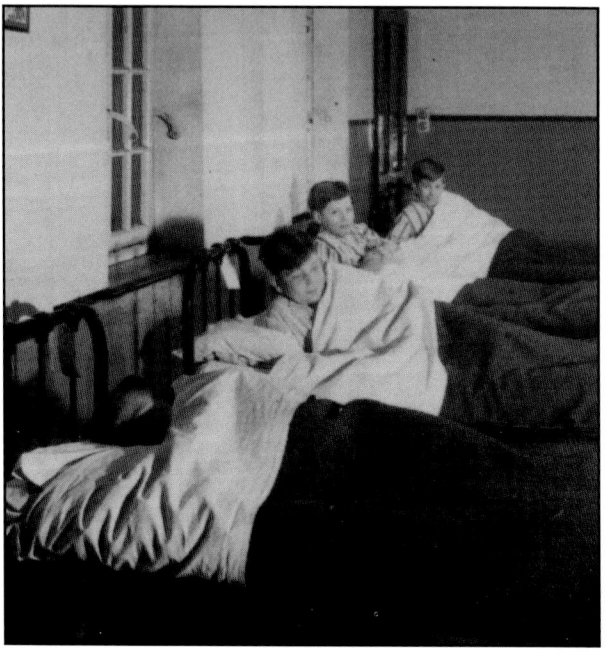

School

The School was independent of the Home. Mr Urquhart was the Headmaster of the School and he was a Scot. He was only a little man with these pince-nez glasses. The boys called him "Nowsie" because, when he used to give the cane, he used to say, "Now see what you get!". So the boys named him "Nowsie".

You could get the cane for unnecessary noise, or if you shouted out in the classroom. Downstairs was the worst; if you got the cane from Mr Bennett, it was terrible. I used to flinch when I saw a boy being caned.

There was also the great day that used to come round once a year - we used to call it "Judgement Day". It was character day. All the Schoolmasters, the Housemasters, the General Superintendent, Mr Walmsley, and Mr Bennett would be sitting around this table in the Dining Hall and you would double up on to the platform, stand to attention and each master would be asked to assess the lad's character. Mr Bennett had the final word, he was the Judge Advocate.

The Dining Hall

There were 12 tables in the Dining Hall, which sat about 12 boys and a Table Boy. He was there just to keep an eye and make sure they behaved themselves. At the end of the week, the best table got a fruit cake. They all sat on benches, no chairs, nor tablecloths. Every boy had to do his own washing up and a sample meal would be: on Saturday, you had hot roast beef and potatoes, which you peeled yourself, and then you would have cabbage or something like that. On Sunday, you would have jam tart, not with custard. And tea - of course you had a cup of tea and just a slice of bread and marge and a piece of cake, which we used to call "stickjaw" because, as you pulled it out, you'd get these tram-lines, glutinous strands, due to the doughy nature of the cake and your jaw clammed up.

If you misbehaved yourself, you were put in what were called "Defaulters". You stood at the back of the Dining Hall. You had to have your meal standing. You got no second course. You had no jam or anything like that and you had to do extra duties. The platform in the Dining Hall was where, if a boy wet the bed, he had to quote his number and give his name. He wouldn't be punished or anything. On the other hand, if he was a defaulter, he had to stand at the platform for so long in the evenings, until the Master said, "All right."

Every Saturday night, 12 boys, armed with pails, scrubbing brushes, a bar of soap and a cloth with hot water, had to line up at the top of the Dining Hall and scrub the floor. Saturday night duty that was and for that they got a cup of lemonade and a slice of bread and marge or something like that for supper, while the rest of us went into the Coronation Hall and just played around.

Chapel

We had to go to Chapel every Sunday morning and evening and, at 6 o'clock in the evening, the boys gave half an hour's hymn singing and, do you know, that chapel was packed, absolutely jam-packed. People used to come from as far as Leicestershire to hear those boys sing.

People used to stand outside in the High Street, listening to the singing. They used to sing beautiful. They used to sing in tiers, perhaps 30 or 40, perhaps more. But those boys, they were well-trained and Miss Brazell, who was the organist, she used to train them. Then we had a gospel service after that for about half an hour and we would have all the great preachers, like Charles Ingles from Canada, Gypsy John Hawkins, Rear Admiral Sir Henry Stileman and Jimmy Bryant, the converted farrier. And then, after the service, we would all go back into the

The Orphanage garden in winter.

Jimmy Bryant, the converted farrier with his Mission Wagon.

Dining Hall, have our cocoa and "dog" biscuits, as we used to call them. You would have to stand at your bed and you knelt down and said your prayers, no heat in the dormitory, the windows were open, winter and summer, then into bed and lights out.

On a Wednesday, you went to the Midnight Service in the Chapel.

Mr Jimmy Bryant, the converted farrier, used to come once a year and conduct a fortnight's mission. We poor boys had to go to church every night, but we quite liked it, because he was so funny, the stories he used to tell. Occasionally we would go out in his gospel wagon, which was for the open-air mission and there was all text printed on it and you could open it up and make a platform. There was a little harmonium, and the preacher would give vent to his pious platitudes.

Although I was really a Catholic, I was not allowed to be a Catholic when I was in Fegan's, you see, and, when I left, I went and saw my parish priest and he said it was perfectly all right.

Escaping

They used to ring the bell when one of the boys escaped. It was like a prisoner escaping. There was a hue and cry and everybody running about, looking for this boy. It was like setting the hounds on a fox. You'd hear the next day that they'd been picked up. They never got very far.

The discipline in Mr Bennett's time was very, very rigid. If a boy did a bunk, he got a leathering when he got back - a strap on the backside. It was always a bit of a standing joke, because the next bath night, the boys all knew who had got a walloping, because that's where you got it, you see!

Mrs Bennett, she was the Matron, she was a great mother to hundreds and hundreds of boys. I never heard her castigate her boys in any way. She knew their difficulties and, even if boys got into trouble, she would not castigate them. That was the sort of woman she was.

The Outside World

We used to toddle along on Saturday afternoon to Eales' shop. It depended on what squad you were in, how much pocket money you got per week, but it was never more than fourpence and a penny of that would have to be put in the collection box on Sunday. You could only go out on Saturday afternoon to spend your pocket money and you could go out by yourself but, very often it was two or three. You would get a surprise packet with, say, a Sherbert Dab and some Lotus, a kind of brown, sickly fruit with hard pips inside and you would get a few toffees: or else you would get about three or four large mint humbugs for about a halfpenny wrapped in a brown paper bag. You were only allowed out for about an hour and, of course, you were back for tea.....

The boys used to come into Mum's shop and, when I was six or seven, the head boys used to get sixpence each and they used to have a pile of stuff on the counter in them days for sixpence, which I sort of envied with my twopence a week. I thought they were millionaires nearly.....

I always remember Mrs Eales' shop and the Orphanage children used to go in there to spend their money. I was in there one day, taking me chance with the rush and, all of a sudden, these boys just parted like that to the counter. A lady had come in the door. They all just waited at one side, let her go up to the counter, get served, let her go back and then they stepped in front of the counter again. They were very polite.....

Mr Bennett with "Bob" the Airedale, mascot of the boys, 1926.

Mrs Bennett with Fegan boys at the Orphanage gates.

Home-made transport in the playground.

"Chariot" racing, circa 1936.

They all seemed nice boys, all "Yes, Sir" and "No, Sir" when they spoke to you.....

Then, of course, there was the Sunday crocodile, wandering around the town. The boys always went for a walk on Sunday afternoons, grey Norfolk suits, black and red ties, Eton collars, black and red caps, always looked very smart. They walked to Calverton, masters leading the way.....

Mr Bennett was a smart man himself. He used to have a button-hole that was always in water: he had a little container behind the lapel that he used to keep his flower in.....

There weren't many teachers there - perhaps three or four and 150 boys. They wouldn't want them to mix with us, specially if we had one or two unruly ones with us, would they? They kept them and they were drilling them and they kept them straight.....

Fegan's boys were very well behaved and very smart little boys. They used to walk in a crocodile. They'd be laughing amongst themselves, but they was always marching. They looked a treat. As soon as they got into First Norman's field, or come along the back of the fields, they let them run. They played football and, later on, they had a swimming pool built.....

We used to go and play football at the Orphanage. There should have been "Home" and "Away" fixtures, but they were both "Home", because they were never allowed to play away. It was quite an experience. You felt you were going into the unknown and you were glad to get out. They were kept under very strict discipline.

Walter Tompkins in Headboy's uniform, circa 1927/8.

Christmas in the Orphanage.

If they were winning by too much (they played together much more as a team than we did), the master used to change them and put less able players on. It was a bit of a joke. The local boys respected them really, partly because they always beat us at football, also because we were taught in school to respect them. I can remember one of the threats I used to get from my parents was, "If you don't behave yourself, you'll go to the Orphanage....."

I always remember we had a barn full of hay in Calverton Road burnt down. Some of the Orphanage boys had been seen walking about down there that afternoon. We had them up in court, questioned them and heard the evidence. There was one, I don't know whether he was ten or twelve, as he went, he poked his head back through the door and said, "Where I come from, the Police would have picked me up six weeks ago!....."

Special Days

Then came the summer holidays: you were allowed to go out for walks, about six boys at a time and we used to go to Humpty Dumpty's or Cosgrove and, when the chestnut season came, we used to go knocking conkers down, because the trees on the Orphanage playground were pruned every year, so that they wouldn't have conkers.

Christmas time - what a transformation! Christmas Eve, one or two of the boys were delegated with one or two masters, to decorate the Dining Hall. It was transformed in a morning. Fairy lights with a Christmas tree in the corner (with no presents on it). About a fortnight before Christmas, we would choose our Christmas and Boxing Day lunches - roast pork, apple sauce, stuffing, roast potatoes, boiled potatoes and gravy, Christmas pudding with custard and threepenny pieces. You had oranges and apples and lemonade and crackers. Later on, Father Christmas used to come in the afternoon. They would distribute all the parcels, because every boy there received a parcel. If he did not have someone to send him a parcel, a parcel was made up, so that every boy got a parcel. Christmas night, they had iced cake with marzipan and then, in the evening, we would have a party, a sort of sing-song. Some boys got up and recited and then, on Boxing Day, you had a special breakfast: corned beef and fresh bread rolls. You had rabbit pie for lunch, butter beans, boiled potatoes, gravy and you had lemonade and then you had mince pie and custard for your sweet. In the evening, you had mince pie for your tea and after that, generally, a conjuror used to come. So we had a good Christmas.

Leaving

It was very rigid but, you know, I have still yet to meet a boy who has not benefitted from that. When I went into the Army, the C.O. said to me, "Where were you educated?" So I said, "Fegan's Homes for Boys." He said, "It must have been very disciplined."

I was happy in the home, but there was always the feeling of isolation; the feeling that you were different from normal boys who had their own homes.

Fegan boys waiting on Rugby station, on their way to a new life in Canada.

The Market Square, with The Crown on the left, & Wesley's Tree in full bloom.

The Market Square from a different angle, looking towards St Giles' Church, with Wesley's Tree without leaves.

Fun and Games

Street Games

There was always something going on: each part of the year had its own special entertainment. There'd be whips and tops, then they died out and hoops and marbles came in and then the swimming would be on. Then there were weeks and weeks collecting for the bonfire for Bonfire Night.....

Winter time was roller-skating; hockey on roller skates. We broke a few windows doing that. The boy next door used to come with us. His Dad was a builder and he was kept busy putting panes back.....

From early days, a lot of us would have a whip and a wooden top, which spun and you had to whip it down the road. It would go yards - a hell of a long way. If you'd got a leather strand on the whip you were all right. If you'd got a string one and the end was frayed; if it caught the top and you did it too hard - somebody's window was going to go. They were a bit deadly.....

We used to bowl and hoop. First of all, we had one with a hook on, then you didn't lose it, but when you got clever, you had one with a stick. We had whips and tops

Children in Church Street. The library is now on the left.

Children playing in the middle of London Road, the main A5 Watling Street.

outside the Orphanage - that was a lovely bit of path. One went through the window, and we'd all run! We used to roller-skate down York Road, it was a lovely smooth road. The residents used to complain and they used to try and catch us, but they couldn't. Old Sergeant Rollings used to stand round the corner at the bottom and when you came round, he got you!....

We used to have our tops, hoops, skipping ropes, all in the middle of the road. We very rarely saw a vehicle, unless it was the baker or the butcher, with their little trucks, or horse and cart.....

We played "Tippit" with a little piece of stick, about 6 inches long. You hit the tip of that with another one. Then you had to guess how far it would go. They used to measure it and, if you were wrong, you were wrong. It was a sort of guessing game....

I can remember having a three-wheel bike with no saddle and I thought it was the most marvellous thing ever. I used to have a navy blue beret with some rag underneath it tied on the hard piece. I used to ride with it; it was lovely....

We used to go "Door Knocking": knock and run! Also, we used to tie the door-knockers together with black cotton and you'd knock on one door and they'd come out to see who it was and then the knocker used to go down on the other one!....

Our domain in those days, was Vicarage Walk, Vicarage Road and Russell Street. They were our streets. We played rounders a lot. Hopscotch, that was more of a girls' game. Then the favourite game was cricket, in the street. At the top of Vicarage Walk, on that corner there, there's a standpipe.

(Now it's got a pavement and kerbstone round it, but it didn't in those days.) That was the wicket. It wasn't an aggressive wicket, it couldn't be, because of all the windows round. It was a defensive wicket, with a lot of in-fielders, about an inch off the end of the bat. A crack round the ear, if you weren't careful. But that was the game. Anybody who started thrashing the ball about was automatically out. Well, you'd get a thumping if you broke somebody's window, when you went home, so it wasn't worth it. That was how we played cricket in the street.....

On summer evenings, our parents all used to take their chairs outside the front door and they used to sit watching us playing on the Market Square. Fathers used to come out and play cricket with us and I can remember one night, my Dad and a lot of the men was playing cricket on the Square. The Dads had the ball and bat off us children and one of them hit the ball and it went up and through somebody's window. Straight away, they said, "Come on. It's time you all went in."....

We lived in Claremont Avenue, which was a cul-de-sac, so it was easy to put a string across and play tennis and cricket. Occasionally, a ball would go in a garden while we were playing cricket and that was six and out.....

You'd start with just two or three and, before long, there'd be a dozen or so wandering around and they'd come and join in and we all sort of fell in together and had a good game, a good night, simple games, which nobody does today. We were always sorry to have to go in about 8 o'clock, we were all enjoying ourselves so much.....

Home life for me was, perhaps, a little different from some of the other girls in Stony Stratford, because I went to private school and tended not to know many of the

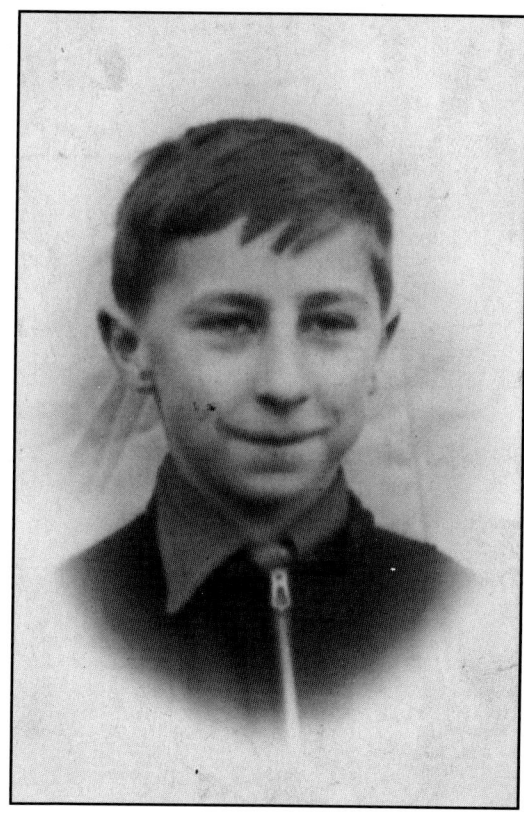

The young Tony King, 1938/9

local girls. We were never allowed to play in the street, like most of the children did. Indeed, I can remember playing with a girl in the back way with a ball and being called in and told off about it. "It's no good going to private school and paying all that money, then you go around with the girls in the town.".....

Across the Fields

The fields were ours, anywhere within a two mile radius of Stratford. So, weather permitting, we were in the fields. We used to take bows and arrows and spears, go tree-climbing and, in summer, scrumping. This used to get to a real crime scale at one time. You'd send organised scouts to see where the best plums and pears were. We never used to do any damage. We never used to take a sackful. We'd only enough to give you a good stomach-ache that day and then you finished. You didn't break any fences as you went over and come out.

At Wolverton Mill, a man had a beautiful orchard of plum trees in his garden - an old-fashioned, walled garden. You used to have a hell of a job to get over that wall. I was in there, after his plums one night and he heard us. He came out with his dog to see what was going on. I laid down in between two rows of potatoes: it was autumn time and the potato tops were over the top of me. The dog never even found me. I'd had a job to get into that garden, but when I came out, I jumped that wall with a foot clear underneath! I was away. That's the sort of stunt we used to get up to.....

Pip Loaks, Harry Atkins, Sid Welsh, Ted Daniels and (in front) Ron Phelps, 1928.

We used to walk across the fields to Cosgrove Quarries. All the children would go there, paddling in the Dog's Mouth. It was a stream of pure water which used to run through the lime kiln.....

That was as good drinking water as any spring. We used to take a lemonade bottle and fill it up with water out of the spring.....

It's still there. We used to walk under the road and go paddling under the bridges....

We used to go down there in the morning and take sandwiches. We'd be there all day. There was a hill we used to slide down. We used to go to the Dog's Mouth, get some water, tip it down this slide and get an old tin lid from the dump just over the road, put it at the top and slide down it. Nine times out of ten, you left the lid half-way up the hill and went down the rest of the way on your trousers!.....

We used to go to Bushy Fields in Calverton Road. It's up by the Humpty Dumpty Hills. We used to take lemonade bottles and go up there and take little picnics. There was a stream, running down Beachampton Road and it was called Gorrick's Spring (The Lion's Mouth). We used to go and drink that. We used to take our shoes and socks off and paddle where the brook ran into the river at the cross-roads at Passenham and Calverton.....

Then, of course, when we got a bit older, we used to be down the Rec., the Vicar's field, it was then. We'd play cricket there with a hard ball, bare legs and no pads. We used to play football down there a lot. There were too many to have teams, so we used to play in pairs. We only had one goal, with one pair in goal. Then each pair was playing every other pair on the field. There could have been thirty of you milling about, kicking one another to bits. Great sport that was. You had to be pretty nippy to even be able to make a pass to your partner, when you'd got about thirty people all descending on you at once. You could get knocked about.....

I think we got all the entertainment we wanted in the Barley Mow. There was always something going on....

Girls swimming in the river at Stony Stratford.

At one time, it was just the river, but Mr Charlie Woollard he was a sort of benefactor, he put up a shed for the girls and just a sort of an open lean-to for the boys. But the boys and girls weren't allowed down there at the same time, so they had special times for boys and girls.....

It was all mud banks then but, eventually, it was concreted round and steps put into the pool and then you waded out into the middle of the river. Then they put a diving board in. I remember one chap diving in (it wasn't very deep) and cut his chest open on broken bottles on the bottom.....

The Mill Field was where I used to go swimming. Where the weir is now, those stone walls on that bend, the river had eaten a big chunk into the bank and that was where we used to go swimming.....

How we learnt to swim in those days, you got thrown in, but they did have a pole with a rope on the end and a leather belt, so you put your arms through that and somebody would hold you up through the water, but, more often that not, you learnt the hard way. But everybody looked after each other. If there was anybody in difficulties, there'd be somebody jump in and catch hold of them.....

We could all swim, because that was our summer hobby. We used to swim from the floodgates, down by the Mill, down to the Calverton Road bathing place and back. Yes, that was one of our favourites. Straight up the river and back again. We never used to swim down the other way, because it's too shallow. I think the river was deeper then, than it is today. It seems, in retrospect, that it was. I never heard of anyone drowning there, but one boy did get Weil's Disease from rats' urine.

If it was fine, we used to play down by the bathing place, out on the field and we used to have tents; take our stuff over there and have our tea in the tents. Then we used to go down to the river and make rafts out of reeds and sit on them till they sank. All the boys could swim you see, because we got pushed in so, if you didn't swim, that was it.....

We used to have little fishing nets. They was what used to come out of the dried peas packets. You'd get a packet of dried peas and they'd have a little net in the bottom. You'd pop the peas in the net and put them to soak with some bicarbonate of soda, then you got mushy peas for the next day. Mum used to give us the little nets. My Dad used to put a ring of wire on and put it into a little cane and we'd have them for fishing and go and fish off the White Bridge.....

Launching a boat from Hayes Boatyard into the canal at Old Stratford.

You could only go one side of the Canal at Old Stratford for fishing. We used to sit there for hours with our little home-made fishing rods. We used to make them out of a cane. We wouldn't have a reel like the proper rods. The float was made by a feather, stripped through a cork and then we used to get little lead pellets, what we used to call the sinker, then the hook.....

The fields used to flood and freeze over for three or four days. I've known the canal to be frozen over for at least a fortnight or three weeks. Some of it was a bit thin - we called it cat's eyes - you couldn't skate on that. It used to break as soon as you got on. It was safe on the deeper water. They used to skate from *The Buckingham Arms* in Old Stratford up to Cosgrove. The canal used to be called the Buckingham Arm. There was a little tributary came this way, where they used to launch tug boats from Hayes Boatyard. That was a big day. They used to put the boat on the trolley and take it up to the wharf at Stony Stratford. Sammy Holland used to run his steam engine to pull the boats out. They were large things, you know. They used to launch it sideways and we always used to stand along the side. We used to get a day off school to see that. Just to see it being pulled down the High Street was quite something.....

Village children was very much respected as long as we didn't get into mischief. We never got hurt. We were a gang together, it wasn't just one or two, it was all the village youngsters, so we'd always got plenty of companions. It was very, very nice.....

We were never frightened of going anywhere, but these days children are hardly let out. Their life is nothing really, 'cause they're missing all the places we had.

They were the very best days that anybody could ever have. We never got any money. Our parents had no money but we made our own entertainment. We really enjoyed ourselves.....

High Days and Holidays

We never used to go away on holiday. As soon as it was the school holiday, we children all used to get our prams and put all our toys in and we used to go down to Catt's Mill to play, down Mill Lane, where it was burnt down.....

I was one of the lucky ones: I had a holiday every year but it was only a week's holiday. A lot of my friends, or children in my class at school, they never had holidays. Their parents couldn't afford it. We went by train, as far as the LMS Railway ran. I went to Wales several times and toured the West side of Scotland. We didn't stay in hotels. You went shopping for your own food and the landlady cooked it for you. Then, it was board residence.....

We went on holiday every year. It was in the days when you had a trunk, which would be filled up and it was despatched from Wolverton on a train and would be waiting for us when we got there.....

The only time we went away, was when we went on the Sunday School treat, or if your father belonged to an organisation. One or two of those organised a trip to Woburn. You went on a bus, through the Park, and you used to stop at a little shop in Woburn and get a ration of sweets. Then you came back to the Public Hall and then you had a bun fight - cakes and things. A treat that was, the highlight of the year, really.....

We went to Mr Fegan's Sunday School outing at one time and they used to have a good do. We went on a wagon to Old Stratford then on Mr Canvin's coal barges, which he had cleaned out, and then horse-drawn to Stoke Bruerne, singing chapel hymns all the way and rocking the boat and we had our tea at Stoke Bruerne and then home. That was a real outing.

When I was in the Scouts, some weekends, we went to Whittlebury Park. Friday night, we all assembled at the Scout Hall, which was then *The Cock* yard. Everything went on the old trek-cart. We used to pull that old trek-cart from Stratford, through to Whittlebury. There was Rover Scouts as well as younger ones. Bell tents had to be pitched, fires lit and then, on the Sunday afternoon, everything in reverse - all on the trek-cart and pull it back to Stratford.....

Assembled at Fegan's Homes, ready for an outing.

The cast of Stony Stratford Baptist Church Sunday School play, 1933.
Left to right: Corraine Hillyer, Betty Tooley, Eileen Young, Joan Hassel, ? Hillyer.
Front: Reg Castle.

John Haseldine in a fancy dress parade. On the left, as a jockey, and on the right with a decorated Haseldine bakery van.

I remember the Fair used to come every year. The Fairs were absolutely wonderful. There used to be chair-o-planes, swingboats and roundabouts with cockerels on the inside and horses on the outside. I used to live for when the Fair was coming.....

Oh yes, Bumpers. You used to stand more chance of getting a lady to come on the bumpers with you than to walk round Stratford. You had to pay for them, but you didn't mind that.....

There were so many things and stalls at the Fair on the Green: they were all on the Green and down Silver Street on each side of the road. An old boy, Mr Knight, used to come from Whaddon, on his donkey cart, and he sold hot dogs and sausages. The chap beside him sold fish, shell-fish, shrimps and cockles. There were sweet stalls and rock stalls. We used to call it "spit rock". You'd see him making it. He used to chop it off in pieces about two and a half inches long and it was brown and white and, of course, made of sugar. I always said they had to spit on it to pull it, that's why I called it "spit rock". And they used to make brandy snap and they used to call that the "Fairing". If you went to a Fair, you'd be expected to take something back, a novelty of some sort and that would be the "Fairing".....

When the Fair came, they used to come in the afternoon with steam engines and horses. They used to line up along the Green and down Silver Street. They weren't allowed on the Square till 6 o'clock on the Wednesday or Thursday. Then they were allowed on the Square for two days and they always had to be gone by half past ten on Sunday morning, in time for the Church Service.....

It was only allowed to stay on the Market Square for so many days, then they would go and all trail up the Wolverton Road to the Fairfield. Houses are built there now. It used to stay, altogether, about two weeks in Stony. It was always August time.....

Children in Silver Street (looking south towards Horsefair Green).

Parents always used to make an effort for Christmas. The things you got were not the modern kid's stuff but, nevertheless, when you got a thing at Christmas, you didn't get it all the year round. You got a good toy at Christmas. We always had a chicken which you didn't get all the year round. The same traditional stuff in your stocking: you always got an apple and an orange, a few nuts, pink and white icing sugar mouse, choc block and all that sort of stuff.

At Easter time, the girls all had their new dress. Boys always something new. I had a boater one year - a straw hat and proper elastic on the inside. There was Easter eggs, but not the chocolate ones. They used to wrap your eggs up in a piece of coloured cloth or flannel and boil them, so you had a pretty coloured boiled egg. There wasn't much else at Easter, except the weather always changed in them days. It doesn't now.....

Entertainment

There was a cinema in Stony Stratford, called The Scala. I used to go there. Threepence it was, to sit in the front. During the War, there was ever such long queues to get in, with all the troops about. There were two houses, first and second house. If you were posh, you sat in the Circle. If you were really posh, you went up in the balcony. You had to lean over, so that everybody could see you, because it cost two and sixpence. Between the sections there was a thick cord across with gold clips on. The one in Stony was run by a family called Moss. A girl used to play the piano then.....

We had The Scala cinema at Stony. From quite an early age, we used to go Saturday night to the pictures. Mother used to like the pictures. You could get in for sixpence and the children were threepence. I recall,

The cinema's programme advertised in The Bucks Standard, March 6th 1926.

THE SCALA, Stony Stratford.

Continuous Performance Every Evening 6 to 10.

Monday, Tuesday and Wednesday, March 8, 9 and 10.

A Marvellous Cast in

Barriers Burned Away,

Starring Mabel Ballin, Wanda Hawley. Frank Mayo, Harry T. Morey.
Showing the terrible Chicago conflagration, the most spectacular fire ever screened.

A 2-reel Comedy,
Starring Jimmy Aubrey.

THE PATHE SERIAL.
SUNKEN SILVER—Episode 6.

Thursday, Friday and Saturday, March 11, 12, and 13.

A novel drama of a policeman's life,

The Man on the Beat,

Starring Owen Moore, Marguerite de la Motte, and Mary Carr.
Showing all the fun and thrills of the policeman's life—it's all in his daily work.

NO NOISE—2-reel Ideal Comedy, Starring " Our Gang."

Special Pictures of London's Famous Cabarets.

Peggy Martin (nee Scragg), outside The Scala, 1942.

in those early years, the first front rows were benches that used to be filled by rather rough boys and there used to be an old man who used to keep them in order if they weren't quiet. Mr Maycock, one of them was. He just walked down and had a word with them and that was sufficient in those days. You see, you didn't have answering back.

They had a balcony, which we thought was the height of expense. I always thought it would be wonderful to go up there. Mother used to take me and we'd have a bag of brown, striped peppermints, which we got from a little shop opposite in Wolverton Road.....

When we was younger, we used to wait outside the pictures for someone to take us in, 'cause you got in at half price. You used to go to the Saturday afternoon matinees and wait outside. Usually, someone would take you inside and, as soon as you got in, you used to go off.

The downstairs sloped and, for about a third of the way down, they were the 1/9d seats. Further on was a shilling. When you was a young lad, you went in the shillings, but when you got older, you sat in the 1/9d, because there was a back row with double seats.

I always remember in Stony Stratford Cinema, a Mr Moss used to let the steam out of the radiators. You'd be sitting there, listening to something, then, all of a sudden, "Whoosh...". He'd do it when the film was on!

On the way home from the pictures on a Saturday night, you used to call into Read's Fish and Chip shop and have a fish and chip supper. If you didn't have enough money, you'd buy chips in a bag and eat them down the street.....

We had a "Gaff". I don't know whether you'd call it dramatic plays. That was down the bottom of the High Street, in a field. They used to do plays. They had about four or five chorus girls. Men used to do it as well. There wouldn't be a dozen in the whole outfit. They used to do two plays a week. They stayed here for a couple of months. They put up an old wooden shack. If it rained you took your umbrella, because the rain used to come through. One play I can remember is *"Murder in the Red Barn"*, another one *"Lorna Doone"*, and another one was *"The Winslow Boy"*.....

I remember television coming: my father was a bit of a sceptic about it. I had palled up with a boy who lived on a farm near Bicester and I used to spend my school holidays there. They had a television set. When my father came over to pick me up and he saw it, he was cured! He was very pally with Len Dewick, who had the electrical shop on the corner of New Street and High Street, so he went to see him. The day duly arrived when the Sutton Coldfield Station began transmission. Len

Walter Franklin, in 1926/7 aged 16 - 17 years, on his racing bicycle.

arrived at our house and set the TV up. My mother said all she saw for the first few days were the backsides of my Dad and Len Dewick! The TV didn't start until 7.30 and finished about 10.30. We had the TV for the Coronation. All the people crammed into the few houses that had TV for that.....

They would have musical evenings in our house, which was about half as big as this one. There was a chap named Paddy Lucas who played the banjo. He had ginger hair and always wore a Panama and a bow tie. They would all come up and do something. They would just roll up when they felt like it. Most houses had a piano or some musical instrument. When I got a bit older and could sing, I used to join in. We used to stand round the piano on a Sunday evening. One of them would play and we would each take a turn and sing.

We used to have a big flower show, which would be held in the Gas-House Field, right at the bottom end of town. They used to put a big marquee up there and it was a big competition. They used to have the Equestrian Riding School from Weedon. They was soldiers and they used to come and perform on their horses. They would gallop along with a lance in their hand and stick a peg that was in the ground and whip it up. Then they would be galloping bareback, with no saddle, and they had to lean right over and pick up a stump in the ground about two feet high. They used to have a belt round the horse's girth with two handles on the top, so they could hold it and they used to run alongside and swing themselves over and sit backwards on the horse. We would clap like hell.

The Horticultural Show was good. They was very hot on showing in them days. If somebody saw you'd won a prize and they knew you didn't grow it, they used to put half a crown on the table and say, "I'm objecting to that man's prize." They used to have a meeting and if he could prove that this man didn't grow that stuff, he was disqualified and the man got his half-crown back, but if he failed to prove his case, he lost his half crown.....

Soldiers on manoeuvres in 1913, marching down Wolverton Road.

Stony Stratford football team, 1928.

We had the Literary and Debating Society which met every Monday in the Public Hall.....

Quite often they would have open evenings and they would have mock elections. I can remember making lots of paper balls and we used them to throw at the opposition, because my Dad was standing. They also had mock trials; it would all be set up like a courtroom.....

You've heard of Arthur Bryant, the historian. We put him on the map. He was a young student and he came down and practised on us. He did a whole winter's session. The books that he wrote afterwards were all the lectures that he gave to us. He was full of fun, he was a funny fellow.....

There was a hell of a lot of football teams: there was the Stratford Town, The Pirates and the Thursday team, who were shop assistants that played Thursday afternoons. Lot of cloggers they were, oh dear, they used to kick one another to bits. The Pirates were a very good team.....

I can remember when the Thursday Football Club won the cup. They came back from Wycombe Wanderers and up the High Street, with a wagonette sort of thing. There were crowds of folk there.....

Growing up

When I was about twelve or thirteen, I had a brand spanking new Raleigh sports bike. I went miles and miles. That was the days you could go anywhere, stand the bike up against the kerb, go off for hours and the bike would still be there when you came back. We'd think nothing of cycling to Bedford and spending the afternoon on the river and biking back again.

We used to have a Youth Club in St Mary's Parish rooms twice a week: Tuesday and Friday nights, 7 - 10. We used to play darts, table tennis, billiards and, unofficially, Three-Card Brag. If the Vicar came in, the cards had to go under the table. The Vicar used to pop in round about half past eight, after he'd had his dinner. You had half an hour table tennis for a penny, half an hour billiards for a penny and half an hour on the dartboard for a penny.....

Sundays, we used to walk the High Street. Everybody did. It was the highlight of the week.....

Up Stratford High Street, on Sunday nights, they used to call it "The Bunny Run". You'd walk up and down, talk to the girls, sometimes, in the summer, you walked across the fields to Cosgrove....

They used to go and stand about in the shop doorways and they used to reckon that, if you walked up the "Bunny Run", eventually you'd get a young man. This is going back about 1936 or '37. It was like a promenade at the seaside. If you'd got a new coat or anything new, you had to appear....

I think there was some people in them days, met their partners on the "Bunny Run"....

Sergeant Rollings would come by. "Come along. Out of those doorways."......

If any of the shopkeepers didn't want it, they used to put a little gate across the front of the shop, so you didn't go in the doorway. I remember Grafton Cycles put in a little gate, so no one could go in their doorway. Oh dear. When you think about it!....

2nd Stony Stratford Wolf Cub Pack, June 1949.

Back Row (left to right): John Roberts, John Tapp, Keith Bailey, John Quinn, Eugene Daniells, Gordon Bradshaw, Geoffrey Pallitt, Trevor Roberts, John Savage, Terry Pickers.
2nd Row from Back: Michael Lockett, Bernard Leonard, Roger Stewart, Michael Leonard, Bill Barby, Barry Miller.
3rd Row from Back: Eileen Waine (Cub Instructor), John Frisby, Clive Bradshaw, Billy Bowker, Joy Small (Assistant Cubmaster), Audrey Waine (Assistant Cubmaster), David Hall, John Roberts, Bill Clewitt, Mary Small (Cub Instructor).
Front Row: David Wise, Malcolm Swain, Sonnie Pickers, Alan Griffiths.

In front is the Pack's Shere Khan (Tiger) - taken from Rudyard Kipling's "Jungle Book" - which was used in Jungle Dances.

The High Street, venue of "The Bunny Run".

The young fellows from Deanshanger, Stony Stratford and Wolverton would all walk the "Bunny Run", as we used to call it. We all used to walk and smile and nod and maybe have a word with someone and nothing ever went beyond that. I suppose, through talking to boys like that, you sort of got to know them. You might have a date with a boy and go out for a walk with him. That would be a start and then it led to courtship. Or you just had a date, where nothing came of it, and you sort of looked around somewhere else. That was a great pleasure, because that was one of the ways we really met boys unless we went to dances.....

My mother was an accomplished musician and she played the piano for local dances, when they just used to have a piano. In those days, girls had a card, with all the dances listed on, and they would go round and get them filled up with all the young men that were going to dance with them. Of course, dancing was quite different in those days - the Waltz, the Foxtrot - I mean they were dances!....

I don't think Mum and Dad approved of dances overmuch. They certainly didn't approve of make-up. I might say, a lady who wore rouge was beyond the pale, according to the family. I can remember the perfumes we used before the War. There was "June Saville", which was very nice and there was "California Poppy" and there was a rather horrid, sickly, Indian thing they called "Fulnana".....

I was a very good girl. My mother once said, "You know, if a fellow says anything to you that you can't tell me, just smack him across his face.".....

When we lived in York Road, at the bottom was Mill Lane. In all those fields, there was soldiers camping under canvas. Stony Stratford was full of soldiers. My Dad came in one night and said, "You're not going out tonight, madam, those fields below are full of French-Canadian soldiers."

One Sunday afternoon, the door bell went and there stood Police Sergeant, Bob Rollings. He stood at the door with an army officer. He said, "Is your mother at home?". In they come and he said, "You're to have two soldiers. We've took over the whole of York Road." She said, "When?" He said, "Tomorrow." Just like that. That was war-time.

So when I go to work the next day, I said, "Who's a lucky girl? The whole of York Road has been taken over by the Army." They didn't believe me. Anyway, great excitement. When I got home from work, in the sitting room sat these two chaps. My parents said, "This is our daughter." In I go and my future husband said, "I'm going to marry that girl." And he did. I was married at eighteen.....

I can remember when George VI was crowned, there was a street party and there were trestle tables from one end of the street to the other, but I wasn't allowed to go to the party, so I had to watch it through the window.....

I can remember the celebrations at the end of the War: people had several weeks to prepare. We lived in a cul-de-sac, with eighteen houses. Come the day, there was a big arch built over the road with flags. The grass verges were much wider than they are now, so we had trestle tables. I can't think where all the food came from and drinks for the adults. I recall old Mr Johnson, he was in charge of the drinks. My brother asked for a glass of lemonade. Without thinking, Mr Johnson gave him a glass of beer. He howled, he thought Mr Johnson was poisoning him. He was only six! We had games - Bill Rowledge organised the games.

I can remember very vividly one thing: it was a lovely day. I really thought that the sun would shine like that for ever more.

Celebrations in Queen Street for the 1936 coronation.

*Left Side: Mr Smith & Mrs Smith, Mrs Valentine, Terry Valentine, Miss Fancutt.
Right Side: Mr Allan, Miss Dobson, Mrs Langley, George Langley, ?, Joe Packer, Dennis Lovell, Ruth Lovell.*

*Left Side: Mr Dearn, Mrs Dearn, Mrs Purcell, Mrs Caesar, William Lovell, Mrs Lovell, Dora Lovell.
Right Side: Mr Fancutt, Miss Fancutt, Mr Fancutt, ?, Mrs Eaton, Mr Eaton.*

Gidman's tobacconists, 42 High Street.

Ralph Perry, ironmongers, later to be the site of Chipperfields, also an ironmongers, then the video shop.

Starting Work

Odd Jobs

I started work when I was about 5. I didn't usually go into school till a little while after nine, because they let me start a bit later to deliver milk as I went to school.....

Before I went to school in the mornings, I used to have to go and fetch the pony up from the field, the Vicarage Field, that's the other side of town. The pony was put in there every night and I fetched him up every morning. Then I used to have to take him to the Blacksmith's, Roberts in Church Street, Saturday mornings usually. I think he used to have his bread from us (Cowley's) and we used to get the horse shod and, about once a year, we had a settling up.....

I used to have to do some odd jobs, I didn't get away with it scot-free. This was the days of the horse and cart. We rented some grass keeping up opposite the reservoir, which we used to call "Half Mile Field", where Watling Way School is now. In the

Haseldine's delivery cart in the early 1930's, with Tom Haseldine & Harry Mallows in the London Road.

Market Square, looking east towards the High Street.

summer, one of my jobs was to fetch the horse down in the morning, 'fore I went to school. Well, I used to ride her down actually, 'cause you appreciate there was very little traffic then. In winter-time, we'd got a stable in Clarence Road. Another job was, I used to grind the chaff up for her.

I had to take the buns out early, 'fore I went to school. Odd job basically. Every day, when I went back after school, they'd give me a halfpenny. I wouldn't spend it in our shop (Haseldine's), I'd go and spend it somewhere else.....

My sister did the housework. I was helping my father. We kept pigs, we had about six or seven. We'd keep one for the house and the other ones were sold to the bacon factory at Blisworth, so they'd got to be looked after. They were fed twice a day and cleaned out, up on the allotments.....

I used to run errands for Grandma Shaler. Before I went to school, I used to go across the Market Square and fetch her some shopping and then, when I came home tea-time, I used to go and do more shopping for her. Her son used to give me a threepenny bit, every Friday. I used to think I was rich then. I used to go and buy a comic and some sweets.....

In those days, virtually everybody had a part-time job, an evening job. Every tradesman in the town had an errand boy.....

I can't think of the School Attendance Officer's name, but he lived in Coronation Road and he was a devil: he was always after you to catch you out, if you was working too many hours. You were only allowed to work a few hours.....

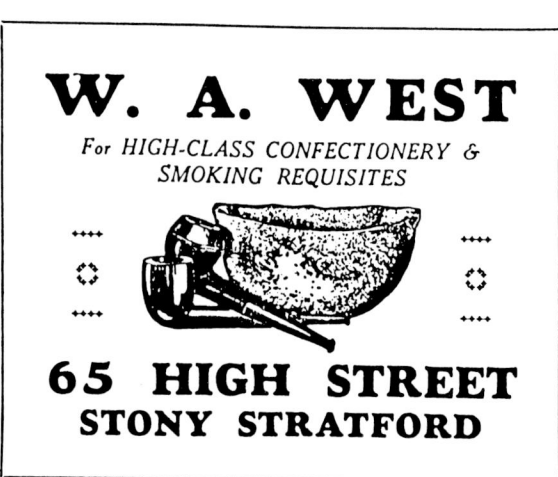

W. A. WEST
For HIGH-CLASS CONFECTIONERY & SMOKING REQUISITES

65 HIGH STREET STONY STRATFORD

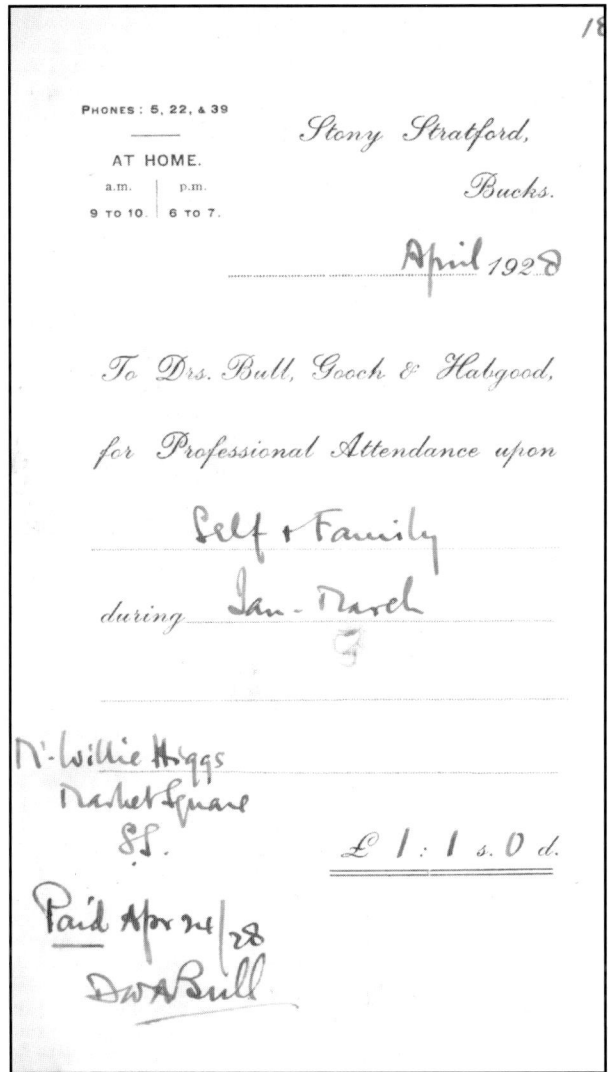

I used to work at the Doctor's in the evenings, taking bills and medicines out to various people. I used to get half a crown a week for that. That was five nights and Saturday mornings. If I wanted to go out and finish in a hurry, if I had several for one street, I'd shove the bills through one door. I knew they'd pass them on!....

I started work when I was eight, going round with the milk with a bloke called Tommy Wright of Red Rose Dairy. He sold milk in Stony Stratford on a float and he had two horses and carts in them days. I got half a crown a week off the milkman and a pound of butter.

After the milk round, it was paper-boy for Mr Bradshaw. We used to go up in the morning to the shop to pick up the paper bike, go to Wolverton Station to wait for the London train to come in. The porters used to load the papers on to the front of your bike and give you a push off. You daren't stop, otherwise you fell off. If you fell off, you couldn't get on again - too heavy. I used to ring me old ding-dong bells coming down the High Street and Mr and Mrs Bradshaw would be outside the shop, ready to catch you when you stopped. I think that was about 5 o'clock in the morning start. We had to be up at the station for the 6 o'clock train. Then, while we was having our cup of tea and cake, they'd sort the papers out and then we'd deliver them. At the end of school, papers again from about 5 pm to half past. It was only the toffs that had the papers in them days, you know.

Mr Toombs, he was a small-time farmer and kept *The Rising Sun* Pub. There was a job there about once a week. Mr Toombs would give us a shout and two or three of us lads would turn up and we'd do pig slaughtering. They used to build a platform of straw out the back. I used to be armed with a big enamel jug and a stick and sit on the seat and wait. Mr Toombs would bring the old pig round and cut its throat on the straw and I'd catch the blood in the big enamel jug and you'd have to stir it until it got cold, so it didn't clot. That was used for making pig's puddings. Then came the ritual of burning the hairs off, and scrubbing them, cutting them and hanging them up. That was a regular job. That was entertainment.....

Mr Toombs used to have about 12 cows and I used to go across and help with haymaking and all that. He used to put his cows in the Vicarage Field. All I wanted to do from quarter to four, was get out of school and let them cows through and take them down for milking.....

I graduated from the choir to organ-blower. I used to have to pump the organ. I remember there was a little weight on a bit of string and, as you pumped, so this weight came down and you had to keep this weight in a certain position. If you got interested in something and you looked away the weight had gone. It was hard work because Mr Toms, the Headteacher, used to play it and, by God, he used to play. You had to keep pumping all the while, so you earned your bob, maybe half a crown a month.....

Proper Jobs

We left school at 14. Most people worked for a trader up the street as an errand boy until you was 15 then, if your father worked at the Railway Works, you were lucky, you got an apprenticeship in the Works, if you passed the Doctor. If your father wasn't there, you just went there as a labourer. You worked there until you were 21 and then you got your papers as a tradesman.....

All the brothers went to Wolverton Works, bar me. I wouldn't have it. I wasn't going in those big gates. It was my Dad's life, you see, and it was their life. For example, if Bill Brown lived in Wolverton Road or Clarence Road, they never used to refer to where he lived. They'd say, "Bill Brown works in the Smithy.", even if he lived just up here. Everything centred around Wolverton Works. The shops used to shut when Wolverton Works went on holiday.....

You didn't have unemployment in those days, not if you were London North Western. Soon as the boys were born, their

Laying the sewers in High Street, from a postcard, postmarked 1926.

Wickins Shop, on the High Street.

names went down so that, when they were school-leaving age, they were sent for. They had a choice of going round the shops to see what they'd like; if they wanted to be a bodymaker, electrician or a smith. The girls stayed at home until we got our different jobs.....

When I left school, I was 14. Then when I was about fifteen and a half I should have gone into the Carriage Works, but I was a bit of a rebel, so I went into private service and became a footman and from footman to valet-chauffeur. Then along came the War and I went into the Army.....

I was working in the Carriage Works, which was about the only place anyone could work in those days. My wages, until I was 18, was about eighteen shillings a week, depending on whether I went out to the Technical School or not. It was about sixteen shillings and sixpence, if I had to lose half a day's pay for attending school. On our 18th birthday, we got a substantial rise in our base rate and we also joined the Workshop's piece-work system, which meant that you took home anything from thirty to thirty-five shillings a week, which was a big jump from eighteen shillings.....

E. J. Wickins, that's where I first started work, when I left school. Errand boy and traveller's boy. Mr Marriott was the traveller and he used to do the country round. One day, it would be Calverton and part of Beachampton, another, it would be Deanshanger and Leckhampstead. Another time, Paulerspury and Potterspury. We used to go round the houses with samples and take orders and then the stuff would be delivered on the Friday or Saturday and we'd take back what they didn't want, or take the money for what they'd bought. I did that for about 2 years.....

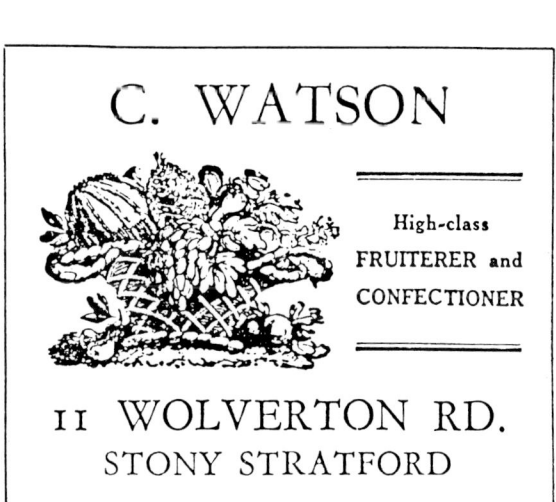

C. WATSON

High-class FRUITERER and CONFECTIONER

11 WOLVERTON RD.
STONY STRATFORD

The employees of Stony Stratford Post Office, Head Postmaster, Sub-postmaster, Postmen & Telegram boys.

I was a Telegram boy, I started at 14. I had a uniform with a little round hat with a button on the top and a jacket with brass buttons, a leather belt with a brass buckle on it and a pouch for me telegrams. They gave me a tin hat as well. I was sixteen when the War ended. An air gunner was shot down and I had to take the telegram to his mother who lived in York Road. She came to the door and, as soon as she saw the telegram she started to cry and so I immediately knocked on next door and walked in and said, "Could you come, I think your neighbour has had bad news." But there were several like that during the War.

Apart from the town in Stony Stratford, I regularly delivered telegrams to Old Stratford and Beachampton, Calverton and, on Wednesdays, I also had to deliver to Wicken and Cosgrove in the afternoons, because their post office was closed. On Saturdays, it was Potterspury and Yardley Gobion and Wakefield Lodge, which in those days was an Army station. But there were about three gates I had to lift me bike over and it was a damn heavy post office bike and you'd get back and there'd be another one!....

I started at E.T. Ray's on 8th August, 1939 and I retired on the 8th August 1989. I was fourteen when I started, that was the age you left school. The first two years at E.T. Ray's, I was general factotum. In them days, most firms had an office boy or girl. You did odd jobs. They'd tell you to go and get a bucket of steam or a rubber hammer. I didn't fall for it.....

I wanted to be a farmer, my whole life was set on farming, but my mother said I'd got to learn a trade. She arranged with Mr Betts of the local builders, Betts and Faulkner's and she just told me and that was it. Mr Betts was a very big Church man and I was in the Choir and my mother went to him to ask him for a job and I think it was because I was in the Choir, I got the job.

For six months, I went with the painters, paid ten shillings for a forty hour week. There was always plenty of tricks played on you, when you started with the firm. They put you up against the door, with your back to the door, and your head looking straight forward. They'd come at you with a chisel and go across the top of your head. It would catch a bit of your hair. They would say, "Walk away," and then nail that bit of hair down. That was what height you were when you started.

'Phone: STONY STRATFORD 11

Betts & Faulkner

Builders and Contractors

Undertakers and House Agents

Repairs to all property efficiently attended to.

•

28 HIGH STREET
STONY STRATFORD

Jim Franklin with tradesmen & labourers, building Clarence Road houses.

Building the extension to the Baptist Chapel in Horsefair Green.

Then they used to send you for "Barber's Pole Paint", striped paint! They'd send you down to Wickins for a Rule pocket (which were sewn on the overalls as part of your clothing), or pudlock holes. In those days it was wooden scaffolding and they used to leave a brick out, where they put the scaffolding in. That's what they called a pudlock hole.

To be a plumber, you had to play the "Plumber's Bugle". It was 1941, we were putting pipes in the trenches to the houses from the Mains. When I got there, they said, "Come on, we'll give you a plumber's bugle to play." They got a coil of lead, which was about half a hundredweight, put it on me shoulders, with a mouthpiece and one end bellied out a bit wider. They put the other bit in my ear, then they said, "Blow". I blew into it. "No, you've got to blow harder to get a sound." So, of course, I did blow and I was covered in black soot. They'd filled this pipe with a packet of plumber's black powder, which we used to black the pipes.

Laying a tennis court.

But I had the last laugh on them: I'd got this beautiful abscess on me tooth. (Well you went to work because, if you stopped at home, you didn't get any money. Providing you could walk and breathe you went to work.) Old Bill said, "Come here, I'll wipe it off for you." 'Course he got his hanky out, spat on it, rubbed it all in. Well, I laughed that much, it burst me abscess. One of the ladies there, she came out and said, "What have they been doing to you, my duck, let me wash your shirt for you." I had the last laugh on me mates, 'cause, the rest of the day, I was sat inside by the fire and they were out in the snow!....

I didn't really want to be a baker. I had to stop home and help, because they hadn't got anybody else to help with the business, but I soon got into the way of it.

Women's Work

I left school at 14 and got a job at McCorquodale's. Most girls did, if they hadn't any higher education, and most of those that did, didn't really go on to University. We either worked in McCorquodale's, or we worked in the local shops. The idea of going into service was going out then, because people didn't keep servants so much.

When I started work, I earned seven shillings and sixpence and part of that, of course, I gave to my mother. I worked with the large machinery. I never liked it very much. We fed in papers into these large machines. A man was actually in charge of them, but the girls just sort of watched the machines to see if they went right. The machines were very noisy and it was monotonous. I don't know how we stood it really.....

I left school at 14 and the first job I got was down at Burton's stores. Father had asked if I could have a job in the Railway Works and also my uncle was Foreman at the Printing Works. I got my name down at both places and also at the Co-op in Market Square, to get in the offices, but none of them had got vacancies, so we just had to wait until something came up. I went to Burton's Stores for about eight weeks and I didn't like that at all. My mental arithmetic was playing me up. The Railway Works came up first and I had to go for an interview and a medical in London. I got a job as a circuit girl in what was the Hurricane wing shop, because it was Wartime and they were repairing Hurricane wings there. The man would come to the hatchway and I would have to write out all the requisitions for the nuts and bolts and the like that they would need to repair these wings. In between whiles, I would do a circuit route, whereby you put so much paper into the in-tray and took work out of the out-tray and took it on to the different places.....

EDITH HALL (Next door to Post Office)

52 High Street
Stony Stratford

Ladies' Outfitter
Hosiery, Gloves,
Silk Underwear,
Exclusive Robes,
and Jumpers

Phone: 51 Stony Stratford

W. Sedgley
and Son
—
ENGLISH
and
FOREIGN
Fruiterers
—
FLORISTS
Wreaths & Crosses
at shortest notice.

Phone: 51 Stony Stratford 27 High St.

When I first went to work, it was at a little fruit shop in the High Street - the name was Paine - and the daughter was living with them, because her husband was in the Army. They wanted a young lady to take the baby out and do little jobs, dust the room, etcetera. Sometimes, they'd ask me if I could do a little bit in the shop.....

It was accepted that, until you knew what you were going to do, you stayed at home.....

Well, I went home one day and I told my mother I'd got a job. She said, "You've only just left school. Who said you wanted a job?" I'd heard Hall and White's wanted an assistant. I was the only girl there. When I first went there, I used to go delivering goods in the country with a fellow who drove the van. Very poor pay, right up until I was married, I only earned twenty-eight shillings a week. From eight in the morning till six at night and, at the weekend, until eight. At Christmas, you had to work over, probably half past eight, nine, perhaps later than that. And, of course, in those days you had to weigh everything up, you see. We had to weigh all the sugar up in ones and twos, and the margarine. We used to have two milkmen, Mr Wright and Mr Tooley, they always used to come for their butter on a Friday. It took us all morning to do it up.

A bill for bicycle & car servicing circa 1928.

Old Mr Hall said, "You'll never be a grocer till you can wrap a pound of lentils." As you can imagine, they slid all over the place, but I did manage in the end. Then there was another grocer, just down the street, the name of Tibbett's and we used to exchange things with one another. If we run out, we could go and fetch some from there and they'd fetch some from us.....

I left school at 14. I went to work for a doctor in service at five shillings a week. You started at seven thirty and finished after their evening meal had been washed up. I had to wear a uniform. They had a cook and a nanny for the children. They had a lady who came in and cleaned the brass and the silver. I did dusting and hoovering.....

When I was a girl, married women didn't go to work. Not in Stony. They might have done in the big cities. The only women who went to work were widows. They got such small pensions that they had to go out and clean. Generally speaking, there was no work for married women anyway, so you spent your time bringing up your family.

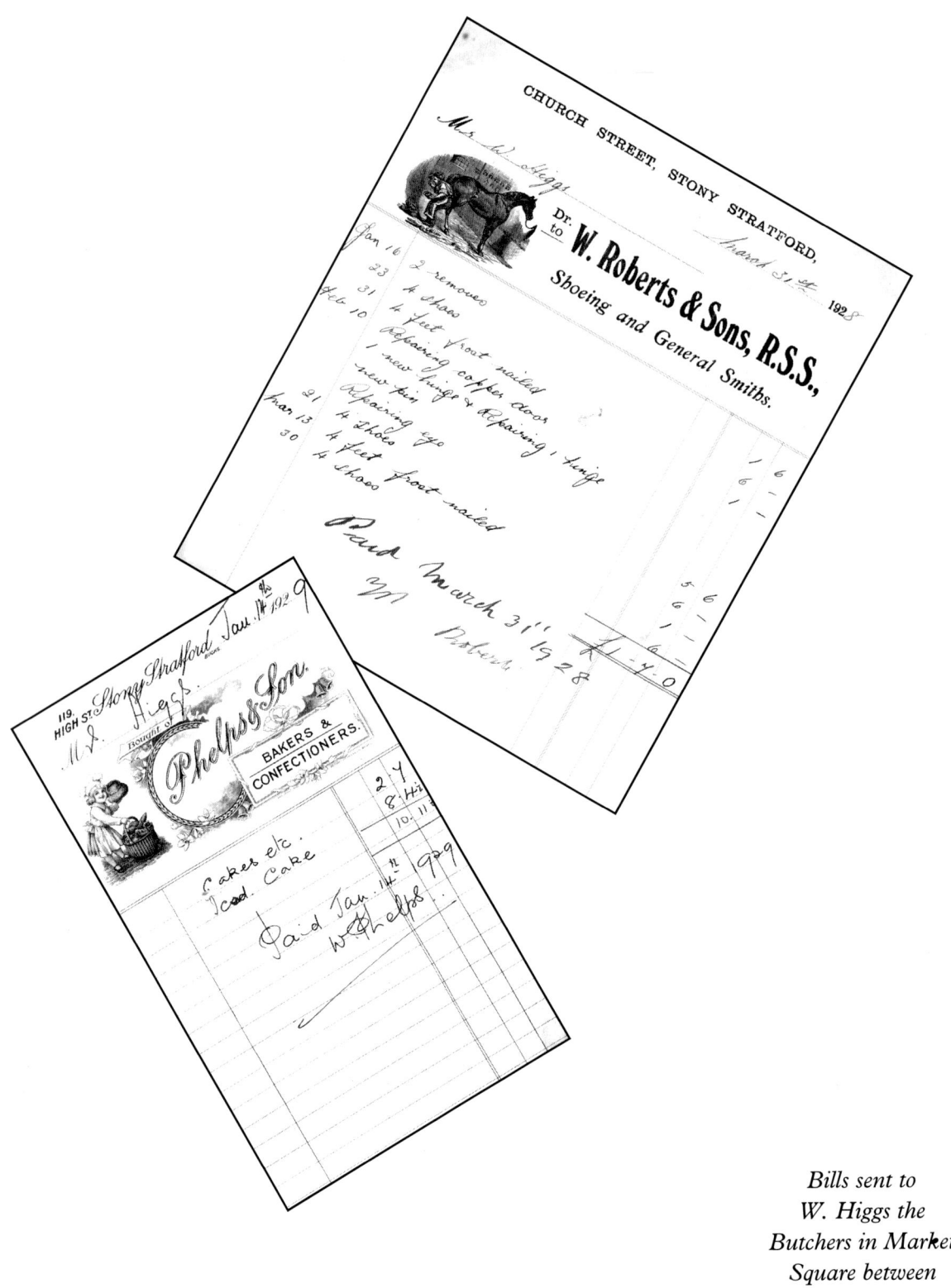

Bills sent to W. Higgs the Butchers in Market Square between 1928-29.

Grown Ups

Shopkeepers and Traders

You thought of nearly everyone up the Street as characters: Mrs Eales' sweet shop and dairy was a handy place to shop, for she sold something of everything. Monday morning was soap, soda, starch and blue - that was for the washing. It was always Sunlight Soap. Soda, that was in a sack behind the counter, next to the sack with the sugar in. Same scoop for both. She used to sell kids' stuff, like "Lucky Bags", which had broken biscuits and that sort of stuff.....

You could buy four items for a penny: a farthing strip of licquorice, a farthing sherbert, a farthing "lucky bag" and a farthing gob stopper.

Next door, was a Rag 'n' Bone man. He used to go totting and they also used to sell second-hand clothes. They were never washed or cleaned. They used to have a pony and cart and that was one house, where they had to take the pony through the house to get to the stable. Leave the cart outside, there was a bit of a passage, then they'd go through a room and then into the stable.....

Wickins was ladies' outfitters, millinery, carpet fittings, furniture, men's outfitters, boot fitters, the lot. Mr Wickins, E.J., was a big, portly fellow, big red round face. His son Sid was just about the same. They stuck out as being what they were.

The corner of High Street & Church Street, with E.J. Wickins' shop on the corner.

Canvins, No.1 High Street. From postcard dated 1905.

You'd got Cox & Robinson's straight opposite him: Mr Philpotts was the manager there - dapper little man. Cowley's, the Undertakers. Mr Cowley was a character too, big tall man with a big moustache.....

Mrs Clarke served in Watt's & Beck's cake shop which had a hole in the window. We used to go over and poke the cakes. The hole wasn't big enough to get the cakes out, but we used to move 'em.

Porky Green - he sold only pork. He used to make lovely pork pies and he'd sit in the shop making them - a tray of pork pies, with little funnels stuck in each one to pour the gravy in. Then he'd walk across to Haseldine's with them on his head. There was nothing hygienic in those days.

Granny Bull's shop was the sweet shop - scruffy little place. She had sweets in boxes, about one and a half inches deep, and the cat was always lying on them. The cat used to be fast asleep, lying on these sweets and we used to buy 'em, 'cause they were cheap.....

I can remember Canvin's shop - that was No. 1, High Street. Every year, their window was an absolute picture. Just before Christmas, they had a huge pig which weighed about 22 score and it always had an orange in its mouth. They bought that at the Stock Show on the Market Square. They would go along and pick the animals. They used to slaughter their own, you see. Us lads always went down to that 'cause it was very interesting. When a pig was slaughtered in them days, it weighed about 22 score. Nowadays, they don't like fat. I can't understand that 'cause that's the best part of the meat.....

Down Bull's Yard, which used to be called Cross Keys Yard, there was old Mr Crick, the Cobbler and he had a shed down there with an old gas lamp.

Mr Pollard, the tailor, was our landlord. We didn't like him because he was our landlord. We used to take our rent round. He had flickering gas lamps on the wall, on brackets, and it was a bit spooky.....

There was an old lady on Horsefair Green, the end by the War Memorial, and this old lady used to sit out there every day in her house door, making lace. She had a bolster, making the lace. She sat in the doorway, not to advertise, but purely for the light. She used to sit there every day making lace.....

There were two sisters, the Misses Elstone. One was deaf and she used to serve in the sweet shop. The other used to work in the crockery shop in the High Street. I never knew how she kept her job there, because, if she came here she'd drop something. Their mother, Mrs Elstone, used to sit outside the sweet shop, making lace. She used to have curls about 6 inches long hanging down. I can see her now.....

Elstone's little corner lace shop was next door to where we lived. There were two unmarried sisters, Miss Eadie and Miss Minnie. I can remember sitting and watching Miss Eadie, she used to do lovely lace. When the Duchess of Kent, Princess Marina, was married, she made a handkerchief, which she sent to her. She carried it on her wedding day. I can remember watching her make that.

There was a lovely, little shop in Silver Street called "The Miss Elliott's". It was half way up Silver Street. It was a tiny little front-room shop. They sold everything. When we lived on the Green, Mummy used to send me down for things. It was a little paradise. That was the only shop down there.....

Didn't matter when you go in there, it was always, "Oh, Bless you, yes." They were always her words. She had a mark on her forehead, where she lent on the till lid. She held it open with her head, so she could sort the money out. They were a bakery as well. You couldn't swing a cat round in the back yard and yet they used to bake bread there.....

My Grandmother was a terror. Everybody said she was a terror. When she was in the shop (Cowley's Bakery), looking after the shop and a stranger came in that wasn't a regular customer and asked for a bag of flour, which they didn't sell a lot of, she'd

Meadows the Outfitters in London House, High Street.

Tibbetts the Grocers, with its gold sign.

say to them, "You go and buy your flour where you buy your bread." She was very rude and abrupt.....

My father was a general draper (Meadows). He sold everything from pins to blankets and down quilts, hats, the sort of shop that doesn't exist now. It was a marvellous place to hide in; the shop went right through a very long way.....

W. W. MEADOWS
General Draper, Ladies' & Children's Outfitter
With almost half a century's tradition for
BEST VALUE which is still upheld.
LONDON HOUSE, STONY STRATFORD
'Phone : 99

Tibbett's the Grocers - that was old fashioned: there was a chair there for you to sit down, when you was waiting for your order. You put in a book, they made your order up, packed it up for you, "Ta, Duck" and take it out if you were in a car. Now, a chap named Harry Horley used to work there and he used to drive their horse. He was grazed in a field behind the fire-station in Silver Street. If there was a fire he had to catch the horse to take the fire engine.

Mr Waite was a hairdresser. I think it was about twopence or threepence for a haircut. I used to like going in there. He had a brush in the ceiling. He used to pull it down, which wound it up, then he'd press something, which started the thing rotating. He used to have that revolving round your head to brush all the loose hairs out of it. Then he'd stick some Vaseline on it, comb it and that was it.

ARTHUR HALL,

MEDICATED FRUIT BAKING POWDER.

THE BEST.

Made from the Receipt of an eminent Chemist, and wherever introduced commands an increasing sale, thus proving its superiority.

THE PUREST.

There is such a rage at the present time for low-priced things, that adulteration is rife. Many so-called Baking Powders consist solely of alum, soda, and flour. This is guaranteed perfectly Pure, and free from alum.

The CHEAPEST.

1/- per lb., or Tins 4d. each. The true test of Cheapness is Quality. Only requires HALF THE QUANTITY of the common Baking Powders.

STONY STRATFORD.

Mr Andrews used to kill sheep and pigs and his father used to repair the boots for the Orphanage. They used to take them over in a sack. Doing for the Orphanage kept him busy, he didn't have time for anything else.....

I can remember Woollards being at the Tannery. I used to sunbathe in the garden and I was naughty, I used to lay there and they used to be able to see me through their window. They used to wolf-whistle me. They don't do any tanning there now at all. It's shut down. It was quite a thriving business, quite a few people worked there.....

Charles Woollard done a lot in the town. He had a bathing place built at the bottom end of the town for the girls and boys and he was a charitable sort of person. Anybody wanted anything, they'd go and see Charlie. He owned the Tannery in Church Street. If anyone was in trouble, hard-up or something, they'd go to see Charlie.....

Delivery Men

Every tradesman in the town had got an errand boy. If you only wanted half a pound of butter, you could go to the shop and order it and they'd deliver it.....

Before the War, there was very little traffic about. Horses and carts by the hundred. There were five bakers in the town in those days. They'd all got a horse and cart. No milk bottles, all the milk came out of a specially made bucket with these various size measures on the inside of the lid, on the rail inside the lid. If you wanted a pint, half-pint, quarter pint, whatever. He'd come to the door with his bucket that carried three or four gallon of milk.....

Old Jimmy Eales was known as "The Midnight Milkman". He wouldn't go out till late evening, with his milk on the bike, with a bucket on each handle bar. He'd come home at 11 or 12 o'clock at night.

Tibbetts delivery cart, from a postcard postmarked 1901.

A milkcart in Calverton Road. The message on the reverse of the postcard reads "Shewing the aristocratic neighbourhood in which your sister is coming to reside."

He'd got a basket thing on his bike which held five bottles. He used to go round with these five bottles, put them down and pick up the empties, bring them back and wash them, fill them up with milk and take them, so that was why he was called "The Midnight Milkman". The handlebars on his old bike were bent with the weight of the milk churns and gooey milk used to run down the sides.

His son, Ray, was the first motorised milkman in the area. He had a little old Morris Minor with a wooden milk body on it and it was a marvellous thing in them days, to see a milkman with a little milk van.

Old Tommy Wright, the milkman, he was another character. Tall, thin man always on the go, always had a cheerful word, always singing while he delivered his milk.....

There was a chap called Don Hickford, he used to push a great big thing and fetch the milk from Passenham. I think the farmer's name was Frost. He used to go and fetch the milk in time for my grandfather to go round with the first delivery (there were two deliveries then). He used to go on the morning one.....

The grocer, Fred Hall (of Hall and White), he used to come up on a bicycle or horse and trap. He'd come up on Tuesday to take the order. The total order wouldn't be above a £1 probably. That would be delivered on Thursday. The butcher and baker would do the same.....

Then Hassells, crockery shop. They used to go round the villages with a horse and trolley, with a sort of staging on the top. There were jugs and mugs hanging on hooks and then the plates were stacked on straw, so they didn't rattle.....

The chimney sweep was Mr Williams. He kept *The Fox and Hounds* pub. It was a very small pub, but his other job was chimney sweep. He used to push his bike round with all his brushes on a bicycle. George Williams his name was.

Mabbut, the Carrier, used to go to Northampton every Saturday with a horse and covered wagon. Nearly every week, one of these horses would start shaking his head and bolt and I've seen him stand with his reins in his hands and I've seen the sweat roll off him. He used to go to Buckingham once a week and Newport once a week. He used to collect and take parcels. People used to put their name on it and put it into the van and he delivered either the same night or the next day.....

Local characters

On a Sunday morning, when watercress was in season, "Cinder" Billy used to walk along the street, with a big, red handkerchief with watercress in a large basket, like a washing basket, and he used to shout, "Watercressio". I don't know what you gave him, but you gave him some money and then he gave you the watercress. I think he then went to *The White Horse* and spent his money. Up the 'Pury Road, on the left hand side, where there is some marshland, that was his exclusive watercress bed, or he thought it was his anyway.....

You could go and pick it yourself, if you wanted to, the stream beds were full of it in Gorrick Spring on the way to *The Shoulder of Mutton* at Calverton.....

Sundays, Father used to take us for a walk. Coming back in Coronation Road, we would often meet "Cinder" Billy. He used to go down to the river to get his watercress and would come along with it in a huge wicker basket and he would shout,"Watercreases, watercreases." He was rather scruffy looking, very portly and wore sort of khaki-looking trousers and an old mac. He carried a basket, which may have been strapped on, judging by the way he had it in front of him. I never saw anyone buy anything from him.....

He got his name, "Cinder" Billy, because of what he used to do: he used to climb the greasy pole at the Hospital Carnival. They put this big pole up, put a leg of mutton on the top. They greased the pole and anybody

The High Street showing The White Horse public house, circa 1910.

that could get to the top, had the leg of mutton. "Cinder" Billy was the renowned character for doing this, because he used to get a lot of cinders, coat his hands and trousers in cinders and shin up the pole.....

In winter-time, I can also recall, as a little girl, they would come round selling muffins.....

Towcester Toff was a drover. He was always in Stony Stratford. He used to drive cattle to Northampton and Buckingham and bring a lot back. He used to walk everywhere, through to Stony Stratford into the Market on a Monday, into the Market place. The Drovers used to take all the cattle away. He was always on call, because he was always in *The Crown* pub on Market Square. If you wanted him to fetch the cattle, he was always there on market days.....

They used to have a Stock Show in Market Square. It was always the first Wednesday in December. The animals all used to be brought in and penned. In those day, there was always a big fence round the Market Square and the bullocks and cows would be tied to these fences.

Then, in front of the Police Station, would be all the sheep in pens. Round the back of the Police Station would be the pig market, where all the pigs would be. That was only for one day a year. It was a market and a show. All the butchers used to vie to buy the best meat for Christmas.....

They used to bring the cows and bullocks and tie them up right near where I lived. They used to sort out the good ones and those who would go for slaughter, the old ones. As children, we used to crawl underneath them, after they'd been round, and we used to take the labels off the good ones and stick them on the poor old ones, 'cause we thought it was a shame.....

Another one was called "Sooty" Nicholls. He come from Yardley. He was about 6 foot 4 and he always looked as if he had grown out of his clothes. They were always so short and it looked as though he got up early in the morning and put his feet right through his trousers. They were always about three inches above his boots. He'd got some big feet. He looked ever so awkward and he'd got a very long neck. He never wore a hat. He used to have a little

The Market Square filled for an unusual sale. Horses from local farms being sold to the British Army for war service in the First World War in 1914.

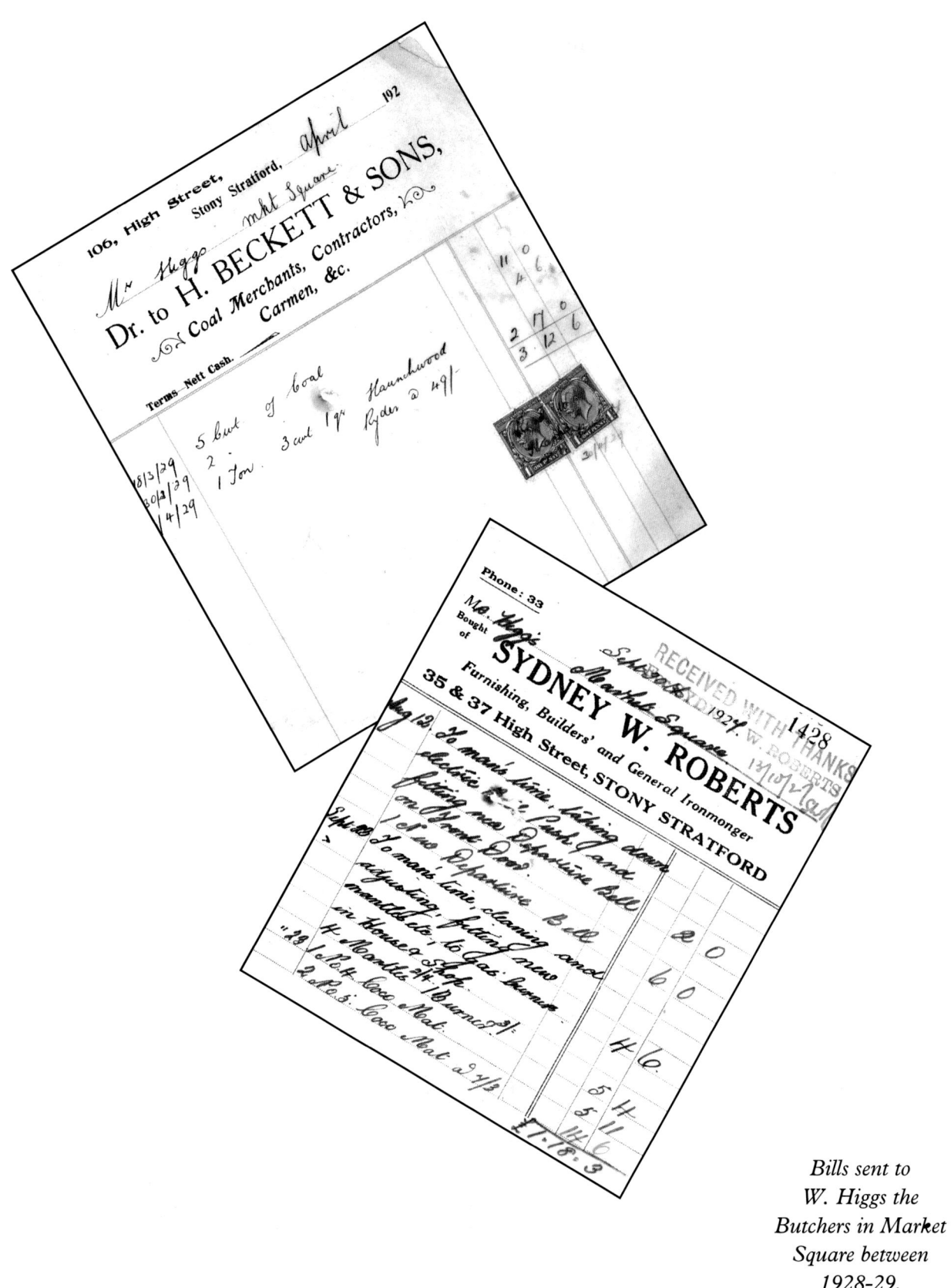

Bills sent to W. Higgs the Butchers in Market Square between 1928-29.

wife with him. She was about 5 foot 6 inches and he was 6 foot 4. She'd always got a smile on her face, some people said it was a grin. It wasn't a grin, it was a smile. The smile was permanent. You used to smile back at her because you thought she was smiling at you. She'd look at him, ever so nice, she'd be looking ever so sweetly. She could never keep up with him. She was always behind him. She'd let him get in front and she'd trot after him, trot alongside him and keep looking up. Then she'd gradually drop back again. If he was going ahead of her, he'd sit and wait for her on the grass verge. He never stopped; as soon as she got to him, he'd get up and start walking again. He never waited for her to have a rest.

He used to hang about here more often in the summer, because there were fêtes going on. He used to go to these fêtes and walk round with a net, with his big top hat on.

People used to throw balls at him to try and knock his hat off. Another thing he did, was laugh into a horse's collar. He'd put a horse-collar over his head and he pulled all sorts of faces. They used to pay him to do that, he was quite an attraction really.

My Grandfather used to come to Stony from Leckhampstead. He was a Teamster, that's a team man - looked after the horses. He used to come in with the bull-cart. He used to come to the market with a bull in a cart.

Where the Memorial is now, on Horsefair Green, they used to sell horses - in that square, there were horses for sale. They used to bring them out and run them down Silver Street. The dealers used to stand there with the big whips. They used to call out, "Run along, boy.", and, as it came by, they'd give it a flick with the whip to see if it would startle it. I think that's why it's called

---

The Noted House for Cheap Provisions.

Finest Smoked Hambro' Bacon.   Prime American Singed Bacon.

ROAST BEEF, CORNED BEEF, SALMON, SARDINES, LOBSTER, PICKLES.

MEDICATED FRUIT BAKING POWDER.
The only really Digestive Baking Powder in the Market. 1s. per pound; Second Quality, 6d. per pound.

ARTHUR HALL, HIGH STREET, STONY STRATFORD.

A Reynard road train, made under licence by the Daimler Motor Co. of Coventry, travelling along the High Street, on its way between London & Birmingham before the First World War.

*Odells the Ironmongers, 1898.
At the door is Lionel Edgar Odell (known as "Leo" because of his initials), grandfather of the present owners.*

Horsefair Green, before the War Memorial was erected.

"Horsefair" Green, because it was always the time the Fair was there, that they sold the horses.....

My Grandfather lived in Stony Stratford, commonly known as "Ridler Jack". He was an old-time builder, lived on the Market Square. He used to spend most of his time eel-trapping down at the old Mill. He used to set traps in the ground.....

George Curtis lived at 20, Coronation Street. He was self-appointed rat-catcher and guardian of the London Road allotments. He never got his facts right. I know he accused one old gentleman of thieving off his own allotment; there was a terrible to-do. He determined that the bit of land by the side of his house was his land, so he built a boundary wall. There were terrible battles over this. He wrote to the Prime Minister and the Queen. Eventually, the Council came up with a police escort and knocked the wall down, He took to his bed and we didn't see him for months. When he got up, his hair was snowy white.

The kids used to call him "Father Christmas". He was an eccentric, lovely old gentleman. He eventually rebuilt the wall and it's there to this day!

We were just about to go on holiday and we had a burglary. We had more money in the house than usual and we had to cancel our holiday as a result of it. When he heard, he brought us produce from his allotments. He was a dear old Gentleman. He loved to talk. If he caught you, you could never get away.....

There was another lad, a local, and we called him "Jumpabout". He used to stand in one certain spot in the High Street and, when it was cold, he used to jump up and down and throw his arms about and keep his hands warm. He used to follow the horses with a bucket and shovel. He used to watch the horses come up the street and he'd follow them. Then he graduated from a bucket and shovel to a truck. He'd made a little truck, which he used to push along. He kept the street clean. One of the busybody women said, "What do you do with that?" "It goes on the garden, on me rhubarb." "We have custard with ours!" they said.

"Blind Barley" came from Wolverton. He had a little dog, which used to bring him from Wolverton to Stony Stratford. It used to stop at different lamp posts and he'd always finish up last but two down the High Street. Then he used to play his concertina and we used to put coppers in his mug. This old dog used to lay by the lamp post and, when anybody came along, he used to get up and stand and look at them and wag his tail. He'd got part of a spaniel breed in him. You know spaniel, proper miserable-looking little dogs. I think he collected more money than "Blind Barley". He used to play about three things and the little dog knew when he was playing the third one. He used to get up and start stretching himself ready to go up to the next lamp post. I don't know how the dog knew which lamp post to stop at. He always stopped at the same lamp post.....

Another thing I remember very clearly, when I was small. You know the Post Office down the High Street, on a Friday, there used to be an old Sailor who used to sit on the ground outside with his navy jersey and he had a wooden arm with a hook. He'd lost his arm and he'd a cap by him and he used to beg mother to put something in it. I couldn't bear to walk by, without giving him something, so maybe we used to put a halfpenny in his cap.....

There was a chap called Teddy Radcliffe. He lived at Potterspury. Funny little man, bit deformed, used to have hunched up shoulders and always rubbing his hands together. He had a little donkey and cart and his job in life was to collect orders from the people in the area, come into Stony Stratford and pick up the groceries and the medicines and stuff and take it back to 'Pury. He used to charge 1d or 2d a time. He used to make a living out of it and everything went well until, one day, the donkey died.....

The High Street, showing a postman crossing the street.

The Barley Mow at the end of the High Street, now a public house circa 1902.

Dropped down dead, in the High Street, outside the chemist that was Cox and Robinson. So Teddy goes into the shop to get the chemist out to have a look at it. He said, "Well, I'm sorry Teddy, but it's dead." And poor old Teddy said, "It never done that before....!"

When Teddy "Donkey", or Teddy Radcliffe, got his cart, he used to stop at *The Barley Mow* for a half pint before he went home. But, as soon as he'd gone in, the girls used to tie the spokes of his wheels to the bars of his cart. So, when he went outside and pushed, it used to tip up. So, the same routine happened every time. He'd go into *The Barley Mow* to borrow a knife to cut the string. While he'd gone, the girls used to break the string off. Lots of muttering...he'd go inside, arrive back and they'd tied them up again. He never had enough sense to stop them at it.

Another thing, they used to tie a parcel up with anything in it, with a long piece of string and sit behind the corner and Teddy'd come out and there'd be a parcel there and he'd go and pick it up and they'd just move it! He used to get played up something horrible.....

There was another old boy, down the bottom end of the town by *The Barley Mow*. He'd got a donkey, he used it for various jobs. That died. Matey said he couldn't understand it, he'd been training it for weeks to go without food and he'd just got it trained and then it died. Yes, there were some weird blokes about in those days.....

Public Workers

When I was very small, we had gas in our homes and along the streets. I can remember the lamp-lighter coming along and lighting them and then, in the mornings, coming along and putting them out. That would have been middle to late '20's.....

The lamps were ornate down the waist and two chains hung down, with a bar across the top. The two chains came from the mantle, one for lighting it and one for putting it out. He used to have a pole with a piece of metal, with a little hook on it and he used to put it up and pull the chain. If the mantle broke, when he was doing that, he had to pull the other chain and turn the gas off and climb up to open the draught to get the mantle out. He used to carry a little ladder with him. He used to put his ladder against the post and change the mantle. Some of the boys used to follow him around and, as he went down the side street into the High Street, they used to put the one in the side street out, so when he went back and looked round to see if they were all on, he had to go back and put them on again. Then they used to turn them out in the High Street.....

The Town Crier, Sid Davis, used to come round. He came from Wolverton Road and worked for the Council. They did say he was very bad on his feet, because he'd been frost-bitten in the First World War. He would ring this bell, which was like our school bell and tell you what time they were going to cut off the water and so on, so that you were forewarned. He used to come round quite frequently really.....

We had a regular policeman in Stony Stratford - a big portly man, named Sergeant Rollings, Bob Rollings, and we children really lived in fear of him. He was a huge man, probably about 6 foot 4 inches and 17 or 18 stone and he had a very red face.....

We used to have a policeman then and he'd be about 6 foot 7 inches and I can remember going scrumping and I came round the top of the town. I'd got me brother's shirt on, with all the apples stuffed down the front and he comes up and he goes, "Undo the bottom of that shirt." I undone the bottom of the shirt and the apples went all over the road and everywhere.....

Bob Rollings was a big bloke - he was over 6 foot tall and about 5 foot wide. Hell of a size, straight as a ram-rod. He was very just. Basically, in those days, we were ruled

Sergeant Bob Rollings, on point duty at York Road.

The front of the Bull Hotel, in High Street.

The Tram in Wolverton Road, from a postcard.

A postcard, postmarked 1909, celebrating the Tram & "Little Billy" the Conductor.

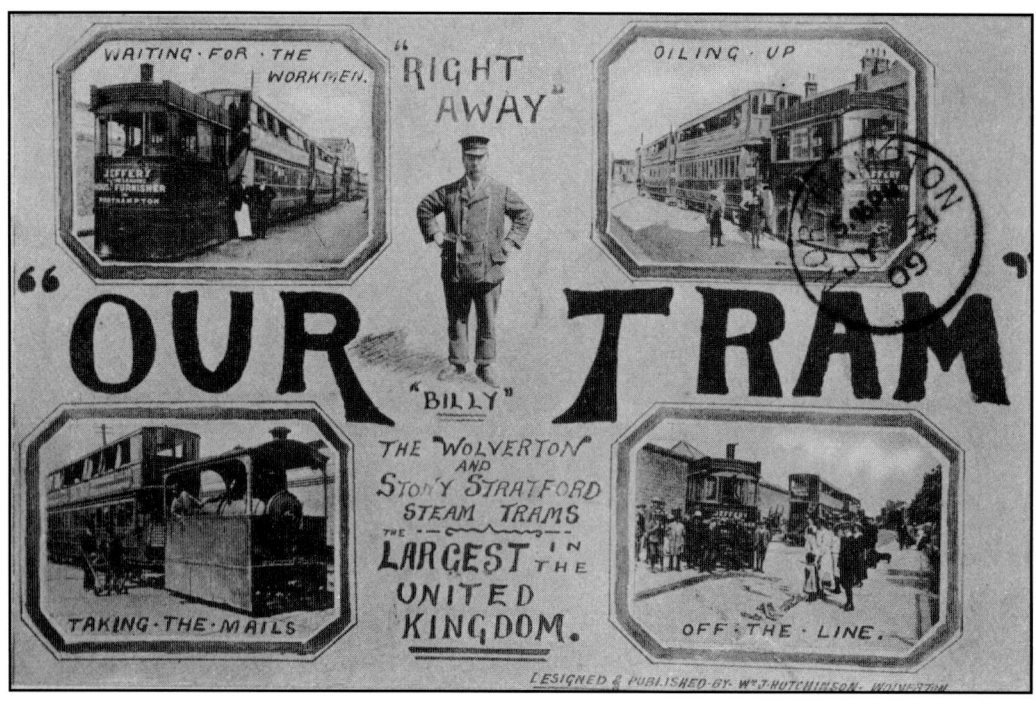

The Tram in Wolverton Road in 1924. Watching in the background on the right is a young Walter Franklin, aged 14.

by fear, no messing about, that was it. If you worked in Wolverton Works before the last War and you committed a civil crime, however petty, you got the sack, no ifs nor buts. You got caught by the sort of stunts that kids got up to, Old Bob Rollings would find you. I swear he knew everything that went on in the town. He'd find you and you'd get a good talking to. If it had been a really serious sort of a do, or he thought it was serious, he carried these leather gloves. He'd got bits of lead or something down the fingers. He used to fetch you a whack round the ear with that. By God, talk about instant headache. You daren't go home and tell your Dad. You told your Dad and you were going to get another good hiding for misbehaving yourselves.....

I had to go round the police station once, one Friday afternoon. I saw the Sergeant-in-Charge there, Sergeant Rollings, and he was going to birch a man the next morning in the Police Station. He showed me the birch and he said he was going to put it in a bucket of water because it would hurt the person more. The man had to strip himself to the waist and lay over a table. I asked Sergeant Rollings had he ever to birch a man twice and he said, "No, once is enough....."

There used to be a little fellow on the tram called "Little Billy". He was the conductor of ~The Puffing Billy". I don't know what his other name was. He was a little, stout man....

I don't know who puffed the most, him or the engine!.....

The dear old steam tram - two coaches and a great big engine in the front....

They used to take the dinners up to Wolverton Works for the men. You'd see them with the basins all tied up with the old fashioned red handkerchiefs. They had to pay so much to put them on the tram.....

They used to store all these baskets under the stairs. Us young scamps used to go upstairs, so the general public could sit down below. If it was winter, you used to have these old canvas curtains you could draw. They used to blow about all over the place. It was so darn cold, but we used to enjoy it.

Billy was a character, a splendid little fellow. I think the days of characters have gone.

Subscribers

1. Sue Starr
2. Audrey and Jim Lambert
3. Mrs J North
4. Mitch Hicks
5. Iris L King
6. Mavis Twiselton
7. Naomi Shostak
8. Matthew Shostak
9. Rebecca Shostak
10. Steve and Zena Flinn
11. Zia Cooke
12. Anthony J King
13. Mrs M Hansford
14. Margaret A Kirk
15. Jeremy Cooper and Barbara Evans Rees
16. Jocelyn Rose
17. Betty Brassett
18. Sue Malleson
19. John Haseldine
20. Alan Rose
21. Rob & Liz Gifford
22. Judith Jeffcoate
23. St Mary & St Giles School
24. St Mary & St Giles School
25. Councillor Maurice C Howell
26. Richard & Isabel Mond
27. Roy Willis
28. E Rippon
29. MJ & SR Chappell
30. Lesley King
31. Robin Haseldine
32. Gillian Whitton
33. Geoffrey Hamilton
34. F Atkins
35. Brian Barnes
36. Timothy John Barnes
37. R,L,A & G Timpson
38. Peter F Brazell
39. Mrs J Henson
40. Radcliffe Trust
41. William Reynolds
42. Mrs J Bates
43. G Ellis
44. Mrs T Purcell
45. Ann Jones
46. Mr & Mrs H G Kitchen
47. Dennis John Lovell
48. Roy Sheldrake
49. Mr & Mrs A P Baxter
50. Mr & Mrs L C Baxter
51. Mark Baxter
52. Susan Haynes
53. O Sucharyna
54. City Discovery Centre
55. Avis Lexton
56. Mrs Jean Bird
57. Mr Ross Ellens
58. Radcliffe School
59. W D Henson
60. Reg Westley
61. Kay Peck
62. Phyllis Hutchinson
63. Roger Hutchinson
64. Albert W French
65. Mrs O Wickson
66. Mrs K V Tite
67. CH & DM Smith
68. P Easter
69. Mr William Gallop
70. Darren Gallop
71. Mrs P Bricknall
72. Mrs Edith Brooker
73. David Apps
74. Martyn Slevin
75. Mr & Mrs R Sullivan
76. Mr & Mrs R Sullivan
77. M I Holton
78. Maggi Clark
79. D & S Pedley
80. Lee Taylor
81. W S Y West
82. Mrs Dobson
83. William & Philippa Prescott
84. The Gibbons Family
85. P L Mortimer
86. Iris Day
87. B S H Egan
88. Betty M Jones
89. A E L Burman
90. John & Geoffrey Brandom
91. Mr & Mrs J E Newman
92. W G Barnes
93. The Quinn Family
94. Roy & Eileen Beech
95. Rib Davis
96. St Giles Residential Home for the Elderly
97. H F Coxhill
98. Ian K Hutchinson
99. R Kennedy
100. Herbert M Booth
101. Mr & Mrs P J Eales
102. Mr & Mrs J T Haseldine
103. Mr & Mrs M G Hooton
104. Mrs G R Hillesdon
105. Graham Brandom
106. Haycock & Johnson
107. David P Gibbins
108. Mr & Mrs D J Clinch
109. Mrs B Langdon
110. Ray Wilson
111. Ray Wilson
112. Tom Wilmin
113. W R Ballard
114. Mrs E J Doyle
115. Judith King
116. Sophie & Amy McGlinn
117. Mr & Mrs C Dobson
118. Mr V Leyshon
119. Brian and Mary T Fitzgerald
120. Gwilym Gibbons
121. Phillip Nightingale
122. Roy and Maggie Nevitt
123. Arthur Young & Co.
124. Arthur Young & Co.
125. Steve Bell
126. Iain Seymour
127. Nicholas Alexander Fuller
128. Nicholas Alexander Fuller
129. Canon C & Mrs Cavell-Northam
130. John Meakins
131. Mrs Mary Fitch
132. Eileen & John Powell
133. Patricia J Brassington
134. Mr T S Rothwell
135. David Muston
136. Peter Green